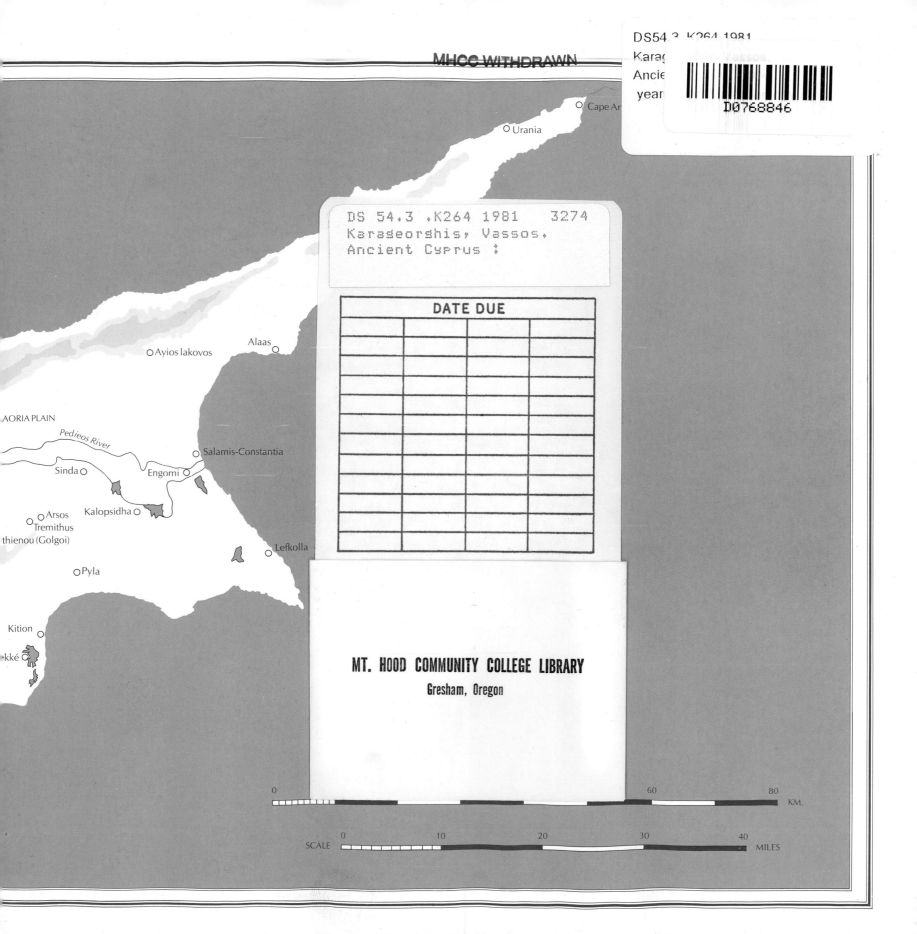

Cape An...
Urania

Alaas
Ayios Iakovos

AORIA PLAIN
Pedieos River
Salamis-Constantia
Sinda   Engomi
Kalopsidha
Arsos
Tremithus
thienou (Golgoi)
Lefkolla
Pyla

Kition
kké

0   60   80
                                                        KM.

SCALE 0   10   20   30   40
                                              MILES

ANCIENT CYPRUS

LOUISIANA STATE UNIVERSITY PRESS
BATON ROUGE AND LONDON

ANCIENT CYPRUS

7,000 YEARS OF ART & ARCHAEOLOGY

VASSOS KARAGEORGHIS

CONTENTS

Text copyright Vassos Karageorghis 1981
Designed by Derek Birdsall
Printed and bound in Greece
by Ekdotike Hellados S.A.
End-paper map by Michael Robinson

PHOTOGRAPH CREDITS:

Nos. 2, 5, 7, 9, 10, 12, 15-18, 25, 28-31, 34-36, 41, 43, 46-50, 52-58, 60, 77,
    97, 103, 105, 107, 111, 113, 114, 121, 123, 124, 126, 131, 132-140, 144, 146,
    152; Photographs taken by A. Malekos, Nicosia.

Nos. 3, 4, 6, 8, 11, 13, 19, 20, 24, 26, 32, 37, 40, 42, 59, 66, 70, 71, 75, 76,
    79, 81-88, 90-96, 99-102, 106, 108-110, 112, 115-120, 128, 144, 147-151;
    Courtesy of the Department of Antiquities, Cyprus
    (Photographer X. Michael).

Nos. 1, 33, 37, 42, 44, 45, 47, 51, 65, 86, 98, 127, 129, 130, 141-143;
    Courtesy of Ekdotiki Athenon, Athens.

Nos. 61-64, 78, 104, 122, 125; Courtesy of the Trustees of the British
    Museum, London (Photographer Michael Dyer).

Nos. 67, 68, 80; Courtesy of the Trustees of the British Museum, London
    (Photographic Department of the British Museum).

Nos. 14, 38, 39; Courtesy of Musée du Louvre, Paris.

No. 69; Courtesy of the Medelhavsmuseet, Stockholm.

No. 72; Courtesy of the Ashmolean Museum, Oxford.

Nos. 73, 74; Courtesy of the Royal Air Force, Akrotiri and the Public
    Information Office, Nicosia.

No. 23; Courtesy of Dr. Desmond Morris, Oxford.

Louisiana State University Press
Baton Rouge and London

Karageorghis, The Archaeology of Cyprus

ISBN 0-8071-0998-3

FOREWORD

The island of Cyprus has a long and fascinating history.
Located in the Eastern Mediterranean between the ancient
lands of the Aegean and the countries of the Near East,
Cyprus developed into a melting pot of civilization and
cradle of culture. During the past 100 or so years
archaeologists have uncovered numerous monuments and
artefacts which are of universal importance as they illustrate
the history of the entire Mediterranean region. Indeed, one
of the ancient Cypriot sites, at Paphos, has been included in
the World Cultural Heritage List.

With a commitment to Cyprus stretching back almost
seven decades, Mobil thought it fitting to commission a
concise written and pictorial history of seven millennia of
Cypriot art and archaeology. We turned to
internationally-known archaeologist and author, Dr. Vassos
Karageorghis, the present Director of the Department of
Antiquities of the Republic of Cyprus, who has been
intimately connected with the island's antiquities for the
past 30 years.

"Ancient Cyprus – 7,000 Years of Art and Archaeology" is
a proud tribute to the people of Cyprus. By celebrating the
richness of the past, Dr. Karageorghis' book reaffirms our
belief in the island's future.

Stephen D. Pryor
General Manager
Mobil Oil Cyprus Limited

PREFACE

While there are several general books on the archaeology
of Cyprus, the present one is hardly superfluous. There is
so much material and information from recent excavations
and researches that a new book was required. Among the
illustrations are quite a few which are published for the first
time, and others which have never been depicted in colour.
Because the book is intended for a very wide public, it is
presented without the usual archaeological jargon.

This book was commissioned by Mobil Oil Cyprus
Limited, and I would like to express my gratitude for this
service to Cypriot archaeology.

The book was designed by Derek Birdsall, who also
helped in various other ways. James Randall edited the
original text. Angelo Cassianos, coordinator of the project
on behalf of Mobil Oil Cyprus Limited, carried out his duty
with patience and competence. Robert Angel, former
General Manager of Mobil Oil Cyprus Limited, and his
successor, Stephen Pryor, extended to me their kindness
and cordial cooperation. Special thanks to Gregory Vitiello
for his assistance in the preparation of the final text. Finally,
I would like to thank Professor J. N. Coldstream, Professor
of Archaeology at London University, who read part of my
text and suggested improvements.

Vassos Karageorghis
Director, Department of Antiquities
Republic of Cyprus

Note on the Chronology

This book was written at a time when major controversies existed among various scholars on the dating of archaeological periods, particulary those of Cypriot prehistory. Therefore, I have included two chronological tables for the prehistoric period which reflect the most current thinking on this subject.

Table A*

Neolithic I (Khirokitia)		7000-6000 B.C.
Neolithic II (Sotira)		4500-3750 B.C.
Chalcolithic		3500-2500/2300 B.C.
Early Bronze Age	I	2300-2075 B.C.
	II	2075-2000 B.C.
	III	2000-1900 B.C.
Middle Bronze Age	I	1900-1800 B.C.
	II	1800-1725 B.C.
	III	1725-1625 B.C.
Late Bronze Age	I	1625-1450 B.C.
	II	1450-1225 B.C.
	III	1225-1050 B.C.
Geometric	I	1050-950 B.C.
	II	950-850 B.C.
	III	850-750 B.C.
Archaic	I	750-600 B.C.
	II	600-475 B.C.
Classical	I	475-400 B.C.
	II	400-325 B.C.
Hellenistic	I	325-150 B.C.
	II	150-50 B.C.
Roman	I	50 B.C.-A.D. 150
	II	A.D. 150-A.D. 250
	III	From about A.D. 250

Table B**

Early Cypriot	IA	3200/2900-2850/2750 B.C.
	IB	2850/2750-2700/2600 B.C.
	IC	2700/2600-2400/2300 B.C.
Early Cypriot	II	2400/2300-2250/2150 B.C.
	III	2250/2150-1900/1800 B.C.

* Note: The dates for the Neolithic and Chalcolithic periods are those suggested by E.J. Peltenburg in *Levant* X (1978) 55 ff. The dates for the Bronze Age have been suggested by R. S. Merrillees, in *Report of the Department of Antiquities, Cyprus*, 1977, 33ff. For the Iron Age we follow Gjerstad's dates *(Swedish Cyprus Expedition* vol. IV: 2), with the exception of the initial date for the Cypro-Archaic I period, for which most scholars opt now for a date c. 750 B.C.

** Note: These dates are suggested by E. Gjerstad in *Report of the Department of Antiquities* 1980, 15f. He considers the Philia Culture as the initial date of the Early Cypriot period, while others, e.g. R. S. Merrillees, consider it as part of the Chalcolithic period, beginning c. 2500 B.C.

I. THE ISLAND

For about 9,000 years the island of Cyprus has asserted its presence on the political and cultural life of the Eastern Mediterranean, which is one of the most crucial areas of human life and civilisation. Yet the island is so small that it would have normally been condemned to political unimportance, economic dependence on its powerful neighbours, and consequently to cultural insignificance. The explanation behind this enigma of history is no doubt Cyprus' geographical position in the centre of what was for many years the cradle of civilisation and the scene of major changes in the history of mankind.

Situated between the European lands of the Aegean and the countries of the Near East, Cyprus was used as a stepping stone for trade, conquest, and most importantly, for cultural contact, resulting in an intermingling that ultimately influenced even the greatest of Mediterranean civilisations.

The island is no less interesting geographically. Although small when compared to European and Asian land masses, Cyprus is the third largest island in the Eastern Mediterranean, after Sicily and Sardinia, with an area of 3,584 square miles, and has a maximum width of 60 miles and a maximum length of 138 miles. Major features are the two central plains: Mesaoria in the east, and Morphou in the west. Along the northern coast is a 60-mile-long mountain range, about 1000 metres high, known as the Kyrenia mountains, or Pentadaktylos. The central and western portions of the island are occupied by the Troodos Mountains, some 1,950 metres above sea level.

Well-irrigated valleys along the northern slopes of the Kyrenia range have offered ideal settlement sites and arable land since prehistoric times, while the plain along the Serrakhis and Ovgos rivers, extending from the inland capital at Nicosia to Morphou Bay, is still the most fertile plain on the island, and is famous for its fruits and vegetables. Mesaoria, extending from Nicosia to Salamis Bay, is a cultivated, corn-producing area today. Its two rivers, Pedieos and Yialias, flow only after torrential rains in wintertime.

Cyprus has a temperate climate and rich natural resources, which won for the island the Greek name *Makaria, or* "the blessed one". Strabo, the Greek geographer who visited Cyprus at about the time of the birth of Christ, described it as "A fertile island, inferior to none. She produces good wine, olive oil and corn enough for her needs". He quoted Eratosthenes, an earlier Greek writer, who had written that the plains of Cyprus were thickly wooded in antiquity and were thus uncultivated. This timber was used for the smelting of copper, and also for ship-building.

Interestingly enough, there is still copper mining on Cyprus, much of it at ancient sites which were long ago denuded of timber. Most of these mines are situated in the foothills of the Troodos mountains, though some minor mines are located not far from the south coast.

Perhaps the most significant feature about Cyprus is its close proximity to the Near East. It is separated from the Anatolian litoral by a strait of only 43 miles and the distance from the easternmost point of Cape Andreas to the opposite Syrian coast is just 60 miles. For prehistoric peoples, who could see the island's green shores from these neighbouring coasts, Cyprus presented a challenge and an invitation to sail across the sea to explore the strange new land. And, indeed, as early as 7,000 B.C., the island was receiving settlers from both regions.

The mainland exodus of settlers from Asia continued until, after several millennia, Cyprus became thickly populated at the beginning of the Bronze Age.

Guided by the instinct of discovery and adventure rather than by any precise plan of conquest, these early immigrants cultivated the arable land in the well-irrigated valleys along Cyprus' north and south coasts, cut wood in the thickly-wooded plains to build houses, and later built small ships and tamed wild animals for meat, milk, and wool. The existence of this first organised Cypriot community was not uneventful, however. Though their cultural evolution was slow during the first four millennia, the discovery of metallurgy and the exploitation of the island's rich copper mines widened the horizons of the islanders and broke the barriers of their isolation. Around the beginning of the 2nd millennium B.C., they abandoned the small boats with which they crossed the narrow straits in order to trade along the Aegean and the Syro-Palestinian coasts, where they sold copper in exchange for foreign goods.

The Bronze Age is a period of interdependence and interrelationships in the Eastern Mediterranean. The rich mines of Cyprus provided an attraction for all those who needed bronze, a new copper-derived material, for both peaceful and warlike purposes. Cyprus, in its turn, received luxury goods of gold, alabaster, faience, etc., from its neighbours... when they were inclined to be peaceful.

If one considers the political and economic importance of oil in the modern industrial world, it may be easier to understand how important copper as a new source of wealth and power must have been for the island's people, and how vital Cyprus must have been for those nations whose ambition was to dominate the region. Add to this the island's strategic position in the midst of worlds whose interests often conflicted — the Aegean, Syro-Palestinean, and the Egyptian, to mention only a few — and one can see why Cyprus soon became the bone of contention among the "big powers" of antiquity.

II. NEOLITHIC AND CHALCOLITHIC PERIODS: THE DAWN OF CYPRIOT CULTURE

The insular peculiarities of Cyprus are clearly seen in the habitations discovered over the years by archaeologists. Unlike Cyprus' northern and eastern neighbours, which possess Palaeolithic or Mesolithic cultures, we have thus far found no trace of these cultures on Cyprus itself. The oldest traces of human habitation uncovered so far are of the Neolithic period, which the most recent Carbon-14 tests date to c.7000 B.C. Though it is not impossible that earlier indications of civilisation may one day be found in isolated caves or remote shelters somewhere on the island, one has to consider, for the time being, that the Neolithic period marks the dawn of Cypriot culture.

It is true that the insular nature of Cyprus may have retarded the expansion of pre-Neolithic cultures to its shores, the sea having always been an obstacle in the movements of primitive peoples who lacked the sophisticated ships of more advanced societies. It is equally true, however, that the earliest form of Neolithic Cypriot cultures betrays elements which indicate an advanced cultural stage. One has to explain this phenomenon in two ways: either it was a stage which developed locally from a hitherto undiscovered pre-Neolithic culture, or it was imported to Cyprus by the earliest inhabitants of the island from areas where there was already an advanced Neolithic culture. The second explanation is, for the present, the most satisfactory.

The Early Bronze Age, dated to the third millennium B.C., was considered the earliest phase of prehistoric life on the island. Then, in the 1920s, a Swedish mission found the first evidence of a Neolithic civilisation on a small off-shore island on the north coast known as Petra tou Limniti. Systematic excavations in the 1940s at the major Neolithic site at Khirokitia, situated half-way between Nicosia and the south coast city of Limassol, opened new horizons for the study of Cypriot history, and doubled its age.

At the time of the excavations, modern scientific dating

methods had not been developed, therefore the excavator could only use traditional archaeological methods, dating the earliest phase of the Khirokitia culture, known as Neolithic I, to the beginning of the 4th millennium B.C. The application of the Carbon-14 method has now added three millennia to the island's past, but at the same time has created problems in the chronological sequence of the various cultural phases of Khirokitia.

Archaeology, of course, begins with people. Neolithic settlers chose the Khirokitia site because it was on a hill, and therefore easily defendable and free from floods; was close to the Maroniou river with its fertile valley and also to perennial springs; and lastly, because the sea was only four miles to the south and thus could be easily reached through the valley.

The bed of the nearby Maroniou river, dry for most of the year, provided the rubble with which the foundations of the houses were built and also material for tools and vessels. The houses were circular in plan, with walls of rubble built up to a height of about one metre, and superstructures of unbaked mud bricks or *pisé*, a kind of pounded clay. These structures, known as *tholoi*, had domed or conical roofs, supported by central wooden poles. Smoke from the hearths exited through holes in the top of the roofs. Benches around the walls served as tables or beds. Interiors were faced with mud and the floor was of beaten earth. In rare cases, there were two piers built of rubble which supported a kind of attic for storage or sleeping quarters, accessible by a wooden ladder. The overall diameter of a *tholos* varies from 3 to 8 metres. These houses were built so close to one another that "roads" between them consisted of winding narrow passageways.

It had been assumed that each *tholos* formed an independent house, but renewed excavations at Khirokitia tend to support a new theory, namely that two or more *tholoi* formed a house, each *tholos* being used for specific purposes.

There was one house or *tholos* which was conspicuously larger than all others. It may have been the house of the chief or head of the community. A roofed passageway covered two thirds of its perimeter, and may have been used for industrial purposes.

The arrangement of the houses at Khirokitia is similar to that of the houses of the nearby Neolithic settlement of Kalavassos (the site is called "Tenta"), situated around the slopes and at the top of a hillock, near the west bank of the Vassilikos river. The shape of the houses is also the same, but at Kalavassos the builders made extensive use of sun-dried mud bricks, sometimes for the construction of an entire *tholos*. In some cases both materials (mud bricks and rubble) are used for the inner and outer faces of the walls respectively. The interior face of the walls is usually covered with plaster, and in one case there are traces of a wall painting showing a human figure with uplifted arms, rendered in red paint. The picture is very crude, but it is the oldest wall painting found thus far on Cyprus. This discovery gives more respectability to the idea of Cypriot Neolithic culture and brings it into line with the artistic production of other Neolithic cultures of the Near East.

One large *tholos* at Kalavassos, situated at the top of the hill, is surrounded by another wall which forms a passage that must have been roofed, as in the case of the larger *tholos* at Khirokitia. The *tholoi* of Kalavassos often have one or more rectangular piers to support the roof or an attic.

Of interest is the fact that there are two major settlements near the south coast and there are surface traces of another close to each other in river valleys, which offer easy access to the south coast. This may be indicative of the route early settlers followed when they first landed on Cyprus, probably coming from the east Asiatic coast.

Another early Neolithic settlement which has partly been excavated is "Kastros", which is on Cape Andreas at the tip of the promontory pointing towards Syria. Its *tholoi* are smaller and less well-constructed than those of Khirokitia and Kalavassos. This is hardly unusual, since Kastros' inhabitants were fishermen with very limited economic resources, as these dwellings are constructed with ordinary rubble rather than river stones. The houses, whose disposition and form was largely dictated by the rough surface of the ground, were situated on the south slope of a hillock, where they were protected from the strong and cold northerly winds.

There is a similar small settlement of fishermen near the north coast, at the "Troulli" site east of Kyrenia, on the slopes of a hillock, where limited excavations have been carried out.

Neither Troulli nor Kastros had walls or other barriers, probably because their small size made them unappetising targets. At any rate, their location high up on a hill offered protection enough.

The rural settlements of Khirokitia and Kalavassos, however, were protected by strong defensive walls. The wall at Khirokitia, which is about one metre thick and runs obliquely across the settlement, was originally thought to be a street. But it has now been shown that the wall was used as a means of protection. During the 'same late period in the Neolithic, a second defensive wall was constructed to include all the *tholoi* of the settlement. Who were the enemies this wall was intended to thwart? Perhaps other groups of settlers, competing for good arable land.

Remains of a defensive wall were also found at Kalavassos ("Tenta"). The wall encompassed the lower slopes of a hillock. Here too, houses of a later period were found outside the wall, a sign that at an advanced stage of the Neolithic period there was considerable growth in the population, perhaps as a result of economic expansion.

The economy of Neolithic settlements situated in river valleys was a mixed one, consisting of farming and animal breeding. In only two cases have archaeologists found a different kind of economy: at Kataliondas, near the north-eastern slopes of the Troodos mountains, where a surface survey has de-monstrated that the economy was based on hunting and industrial activity; and at Cape Andreas, where as already mentioned, the basic occupation of the inhabitants was fishing, as is indicated by the many fishing implements unearthed, as well as by fishbones and seashells found on the floors of the houses.

Carbonised grain has been found in the Khirokitia houses. Sickle blades of flint, querns and grinders also testify that farming was the principal occupation of the population. The presence of flint arrow-heads indicated that their diet was supplemented by meat from animals which were hunted in the woods. These included fallow deer, whose antlers have been found in the excavations. Lentils, beans and peas provided variety in the Khirokitian diet. Animals such as sheep, goats and pigs must have been domesticated for their meat, milk and wool. These may have been introduced by colonists from Anatolia who crossed the narrow straits in small boats. Cattle, however, were too heavy to load on small boats; it only became feasible to transport these heavy beasts during the Early Bronze Age, when sturdy ships were available.

Among the Neolithic tools we found, apart from sickles and blades of flint and axe heads or andesite chisels, were blades of dark grey obsidian, a volcanic glass which, when skilfully cut, provides razor-sharp blades for skinning animals and even for cutting leather or wood. But obsidian is not found in the geological strata of Cyprus. Scientific analysis has shown that it was imported from central Anatolia —yet another clue to the origin of at least some of the early Neolithic colonists. One may attribute several other materials, such as carnelian, green stone, mother-of-pearl, the use of dentalia for necklaces, etc., to these settlers. Several bone tools and needles have also been found. There must have been tools of wood but these have not survived.

The commonest utensils used in early Neolithic houses were vessels of stone, namely bowls made of andesite or other grey stones which were readily available in nearby riverbeds. By skilfully and patiently rubbing one stone on the other, Neolithic settlers produced bowls with open spouts, string-hole handles, relatively thin walls, and polished surfaces which sometimes bore an incised or relief decoration. There were also, no doubt, receptacles of wood and leather but these, naturally, have not survived.

Andesite and sometimes clay were used to produce idols shaped like human figures. Apart from a head of unbaked clay, which betrays naturalistic trends in the rendering of the facial characteristics, the stone idols are crude, violin-shaped objects, or have flat rectangular bodies. Their nearest parallels may be found in the Cyclades and in Anatolia. The sex is not depicted, nor is there any indication of arms and legs. Facial expressions are simple in the extreme, with only the eyes, mouth and nose indicated.

The purpose these stone and clay idols served is unclear. Did they have a funerary significance, or were they simply the result of the artistic instincts of the Khirokitians, who would creatively use their spare time after they had finished work in the fields? And what artists or craftsmen made vases and idols with such delicate finishes? Were their creators women who stayed at home while the men were cultivating the fields or hunting? Some of the idols are *protomes* (heads and necks) of animals, perhaps used as the heads of sceptres.

A surface find near Mari, not far from Kalavassos, shows a quadruped in andesite. The artist took an oblong polished river stone, and by carving the surface, rendered a body with four short legs, head and tail. Now that modern art has taught us to appreciate simple (but not simplistic) forms, the early Neolithic sculpture of Cyprus deserves a good place in the history of primitive art.

Apart from their artistic disposition, the Khirokitians, and this applies also to the inhabitants of Kalavassos, also had some form of religious life, based on the fear, and hence the venera-tion, of the dead. No doubt dying must have impressed primitive man as much as it does modern man. The Khirokitians believed that the dead did not simply perish but would be resurrected in a second life. Therefore it was important to be on good terms with the deceased by appeasing their souls with libations. Bodies were buried inside the house beneath the floor or just outside, in shallow pits. The body was placed in a contracted position, so that it would take up the minimum amount of space. Libations were offered through a hole above the skull.

Gifts were buried with the dead relative. These included necklaces and pendants for women and also stone bowls which were ceremoniously broken during the funeral. Even so, the living took no chances. Fearing that the dead might rise and cause them harm, they placed a heavy stone or quern on the chest or the head of the corpse. There is usually one body per grave, though in excavations dating to later periods, two skeletons were often found, usually of a woman and an infant (infant mortality was quite high, as might be expected in a primitive society). Some of these burial customs are also found in the Levant, and this may be yet another indication of the origin of some of the settlers. What is difficult to determine is racial origin through craniological measurements. This is because skulls were artificially deformed, probably —as was the case with New World Mayan Indians —for cosmetic reasons.

These sites belong to the early phase of the Neolithic culture, known as Neolithic I. They are characterised by the absence of any pottery, except in cases like those at Khirokitia, where the culture continues into the second Neolithic period, known as Neolithic II.

The first Neolithic period may have ended, not because of a catastrophe, but due to a natural decline, after a lapse of about 1,000 years. Scientists place the end of the Neolithic I period at around c.6000 B.C. The beginning of Neolithic II has been dated by Carbon-14 to c.4500 B.C., a fact which leaves a gap of about

1,500 years unaccounted for. Is this gap real, caused by a decline of the early Neolithic culture and an abandonment of Cyprus? Or is it artificial —that is, due to the lack of continuous habitation of the sites which have so far been excavated?

It is hard to believe that sites like Khirokitia, where at least three habitation layers have so far been found during recent excavations by a French team, will not one day provide a continuous sequence. To suggest that the site at Khirokitia was abandoned in c.6000 B.C. and then reoccupied —after a period of 1500 years! —is, to say the least, unrealistic. At any rate, the chronological gap is partly explained by a site called "Agridhi", located in the central part of Cyprus, at Dhali. It is here, on the south banks of the Yialias river, that recent excavations have unearthed pottery dated by Carbon-14 to c.5310 B.C.

Whatever happened between 600 B.C. and 4500 B.C., one thing is clear: The year 4500 B.C. heralds a new phase in Neolithic culture, a phase introduced by newcomers. They chose sites near the coast, or inland, where they built fortified settlements. As was the case with Early Neolithic settlements, it is probable that the walled towns were erected to protect those who had arable land from those who did not.

One of the major sites from this period is site "Vrysi", at Ayios Epiktitos. Situated on a headland on the north coast, east of Kyrenia, the site consists of uneven ground that slopes abruptly down to the shore —a fact which dictated irregular plans for the houses. A V-shaped ditch was dug to cut off the headland from inland areas. Soon, however, perhaps as a result of prolonged periods of peace, this ditch no longer served a defensive purpose. It was filled in and houses were built over it.

The dwellings were initially built of timber, but later on the inhabitants built structures of stone and *pisé*. The floor was sunken into the rock, thus giving the impression of partly subterranean habitations. The interiors were often divided into smaller compartments by wooden beams. Timber was also used for the sloping roofs and for bracing thin walls, preserved

to a height of three metres. However, this does not mean that the houses were actually three metres tall, since each time the floor was raised, a new wall would be built on top of the older one.

Hearths and benches on earthern floors are common features of these houses, as are stone tools and pottery. In one case two small pillar-shaped stones were found, covered with fibrous plaiting. One of them looks like a phallus and may have been used as a cult symbol. This was an exciting find, since it may herald a new element in the prehistoric religion of Cyprus —the idea of fertility, which was a predominant theme of artisans during the next period, the Chalcolithic.

Philia ("Drakos") is another major Neolithic II site, and is situated on elevated ground, west of Nicosia. Recent excavations revealed houses, mostly rectangular, with rounded corners, built of rubble and *pisé*. The settlement was fortified by a wall and a ditch. As was the case at Vrysi, the defences fell into disuse during a later period, probably because they were no longer needed. Special features at Philia-Drakos are subterranean chambers and channels. Were they storage places, places of refuge, or did they serve as primitive industrial quarters? No satisfactory explanation has yet been found. Similar enigmatic features appear in the Chalcolithic period (a period in which both stone and copper implements were used) at Kalavassos ("Ayious"), near the south coast. A chamber tomb was found within the boundaries of the settlement, but there were no gifts in association with the skeletal remains. The architecture also presents interesting peculiarities. The houses consist of pits, partly sunken into the rock surface, with a wooden structure around the edge of the pit and a central pole to support the roof. The layout is similar to that found in Beersheba in Palestine —a place from which some of the Neolithic II settlers may have originated.

The most remarkable of all the Neolithic II settlements, however, is that of Sotira, again near the south coast, where 47 dwellings were unearthed. The houses are built at the top and around the slopes of a hill. Unlike the light structures of Kalavassos A, these houses are solidly built with rubble and mud bricks. They are mostly rectangular with rounded corners, but other shapes (circular, oval, irregular) also occur. A central pole supported the roof. On the floors were the usual hearths and benches along the walls, and some of the houses had partitions which provided working space. There was a separate cemetery for the dead, at the foot of the hill. Burial customs are the same as those practised during the Neolithic I period.

Several Carbon-14 dates have been obtained for the Neolithic II sites discussed here. Ayios Epiktitos-Vrysi has been dated to c.4660 B.C., Philia-Drakos to c.5310 B.C., Sotira to c.4350 B.C., with a date for the abandonment of the settlement set at c.3800 B.C. There is also evidence that these Neolithic II settlements were destroyed by an earthquake c.3800 B.C.

The inhabitants of the Neolithic II settlements were farmers, but they domesticated animals for meat and milk, and supplemented their diet with food obtained through fishing and hunting. The major innovation in their artistic production was pottery. Most of the pottery at Ayios Epiktitos-Vrysi consists of large spouted bowls with bold painted motifs, such as large reserved circles, horizontal or vertical rows of festoons, ripples and strokes of a dark red or brown colour. Similar pottery has been found at Philia-Drakos. On the south coast, the prevailing style of pottery decoration is the so-called "combed ware". The surface of the vases, mainly large bowls and bottles, was covered with a thick slip of dark red or brown paint, part of which was scraped off with a comb-shaped tool before firing.

Slow but steady and significant progress in art and architecture was achieved by the Cypriots during the 3,000 years of the Neolithic period. New styles of architecture, stone sculpture, the invention of pottery and a variety of styles of decoration — all these form the cultural background Cyprus brought to the next archaeological period, the Chalcolithic. The continuous influx of colonists from various parts of the Near East during the Neolithic II period renewed the old population stock and prepared Cyprus to enter the great period of the Bronze Age as a heavily populated country.

The transition from the Neolithic II to the Chalcolithic I period was a peaceful but well-defined one. After the destruction by earthquake of the Neolithic II settlements, new sites were chosen by the population, which in the meantime must have been renewed by newcomers, probably from the south coast of Anatolia. A major change in the pattern of settlement occurred during this period: The western part of the island, which was uninhabited during the Neolithic period, now became the most prominent part of the island.

Erimi, near the south-western coast, was the first Chalcolithic settlement to be excavated. Its houses continue the Neolithic tradition. They are round, but have sunken floors similar to those found at Kalavassos A. The dead are buried as they were during the Early Neolithic period, an indication that some of the old Neolithic stock in the population still lingered on. Further to the west, north of Paphos, lies the settlement of Lemba ("Lakkous"), where recent excavations have brought to light a number of large *tholoi*, which like those found at Erimi are built with rubble topped with reeds and daub. One of these houses, which had a plastered floor, may have been used as a cult place, as a limestone statuette of a nude female figure was found in it.

Tools of stone, querns and other implements found on the floors of the houses indicate industrial activity, though farming and fishing may have been the main occupations of the Chalcolithic inhabitants.

A copper chisel and a copper fishing hook found at Lakkous justify the name "Chalcolithic", which means stone-copper age. A copper chisel from Erimi and a copper spiral from Souskiou, near Palaepaphos, complete the list of metallic objects known so far from this period. Several pit graves were found in a house at Lakkous. Most of the graves contained the skeletons of infants and gifts associated with the burials. The pits were covered with slabs which were perforated so that libations could be poured in honour of the dead. As the house dates to a slightly later period than the burials in it, the dwelling may be considered a boundary for a burial ground.

On a plateau east of Kalavassos-Tenta, known as Kalavassos-Ayious, recent excavations have uncovered several subterranean channels similar to those found at Philia ("Drakos"). Vases and tools found on their floors show that they were used at some stage, perhaps as workshops, but no satisfactory explanation for them has yet been given.

A truly exciting discovery was made at Souskiou, near Palaepaphos. We found a large cemetery with proper tombs that was completely separated from the settlement — the first such discovery dated to the prehistory of Cyprus. The tombs are hewn from rock and are bottle-shaped, narrowing towards the top. Their depth is about 2.00m. and their diameter at the bottom is 1.20 to 1.5m. The top opening, the "neck" of the bottle, 75-90m. in diameter, is covered with a slab. The dead were buried in a contracted position with various gifts. After the burial the entire tomb was sealed with soil and covered with a stone slab.

The art of this period is considerably lively. The prevalent style in pottery is called "Red-on-White", as red abstract and vegetal motifs are applied on the white grounds of vases. The repertory of forms is very rich and includes bowls of various sizes and types. Some of them are more than 50 cm. deep and were used for storage. There are also bottles with pointed bases that could be set into pits on the earthen floors of houses, and even unusual composite vessels, which consist of three interconnected bottles.

The appearance of vases known as *askoi* in the form of birds or quadrupeds is a novelty in ceramic production during this period. One of these vessels, from Souskiou, has the body of a quadruped and the head of a human figure, and thus may be considered the distant predecessor of the Greek centaur. An extraordinary statue, said to have been found at Souskiou, is by far the largest terracotta human figure from the Chalcolithic period found thus far. It is 36cm. high, is hollow, and is seated on a low stool. The facial expression is grotesque, with a half-open mouth; both arms are bent to support the head. Through a perforation at the top of the head one may pour a liquid which flows through the conspicuous tubular penis. This may have been a ritual act, connected with fertility. After being illegally exported to Europe, the statue was repatriated and is now exhibited in the Pierides Foundation Museum in Larnaca.

A much smaller terracotta statuette, in a similar attitude, known as "the thinker", was found in the Balkans. Whether the "centaur" and the statue in the Pierides Foundation Museum link Cyprus with the Balkan region is difficult to say.

One of the Lemba houses, which has a plastered floor, may have been used from time to time as a cult place, as a limestone statue of a nude female figure was found inside it. The Lemba statue, 36cm. high, represents a standing nude in a frontal attitude. Breasts and genitals are clearly marked with grooves. The neck is elongated and facial characteristics are very simplified. Another limestone statue, perhaps also from the Paphos region, found its way illicitly into an unknown private collection in Europe a few years ago. It is 39cm. high, cruciform, and has schematized breasts like those of the Lemba statue.

Such large statues may have served as cult figures for a fertility goddess, as it is known that a number of other small terracotta nudes with conspicuously grooved genitals served this purpose. Another small terracotta statue in the Louvre represents a seated female with a large bowl on her lap. In a gesture of ritual significance, she presses her tattooed breasts to cause milk to flow into the bowl. The fertility divinity is now prominent (a stone phallus from Souskiou, found in a tomb, provides supporting evidence for the fertility idea) and with the death divinity, constitutes the core of prehistoric Cypriot religion for several millennia.

The best known artistic production of the Chalcolithic period, however, is that of the small steatite figurines. Steatite or soapstone in various colours (black, light green, grey) is indigenous to Cyprus, particularly in the south-western part of the island. The figurines are small, from 5 to 15cm. in height, and have a cruciform shape with long necks, straight arms, and legs delineated by deep grooves. Facial characteristics are very simplified. While some of these figurines are female, with small breasts, only one male is known; in the vast majority no sex is indicated. Some of the figurines consist of double figures arranged like a cross; others show one figure standing on the head of another. Several tiny cruciform figures, obviously used as pendants, were found in a tomb at Souskiou, in association with dentalia (seashells) which formed "beads" for necklaces.

1 *(page 17)*

Aerial view of the Neolithic settlement of Khirokitia, near the south coast. Its circular houses (*tholoi*) are built on the slopes of a hill, near a river, a perennial spring and a nearby valley where there is good arable land. The site was first inhabited in the 7th millennium B.C. and was abandoned in the 4th millennium B.C. Its inhabitants were farmers who had by this time already tamed several wild animals. The houses consisted of one or more *tholoi*; the lower parts of their walls were built of rubble; the upper parts of were clay and brick, and the houses had conical roofs. They buried their dead inside their houses, below the floor, or just outside. The settlement was fortified with a defensive wall.

The first excavations at Khirokitia were conducted in 1936-1939, and 1946 by the Cyprus Department of Antiquities. A new era of excavations was begun in 1976 by a French mission.

2

Stone bowl from the Neolithic settlement of Khirokitia. The bowl is made of dark grey andesite, a kind of stone which is found in abundance in a nearby riverbed. The tools used to shape such vases were other similar stones. This bowl is rectangular in shape, with an open spout at the rim of one of its short sides. Its long sides are decorated in the middle with dots in relief arranged in the form of a cross; the short side on either side of the spout is decorated with parallel chevrons in relief. There are two perforations on one of the long sides, indicating an ancient repair.

Neolithic I period. Cyprus Museum, Nicosia, no. 813. Height: 10 cm.; length: 30.5 cm.; maximum width: 27.5 cm.

3

Apart from tools and kitchen utensils, the Neolithic Cypriots produced works of art, either in relation to religious ritual or just for their own sake. These were usually made of andesite and represented the human figure or heads of human figures, rendered in a very simplified form. Occasionally there were protomes of animals or whole quadrupeds. This idol represents a flattened human head supported on a long cylindrical neck. The eyebrows and nose are rendered in relief, the eyes are grooved. Such figures evoke trends in contemporary sculpture.

Probably of the Neolithic II period. From Omodos, a mountain village in western Cyprus. Cyprus Museum, Nicosia, no. 1948/V-17/2. Height: 13.7 cm.

4

Idol of grey andesite, from Khirokitia. It was found on the floor of one of the houses. This idol is more complete than the one in figure 3. It consists of a flat rectangular torso without arms, supported on two crudely rendered legs separated from one another by a vertical groove. The relatively small head is supported by a cylindrical neck. The eyes and the mouth are rendered by depressions. It is not easy to say whether these idols represented deceased persons or a divinity; they may even be considered simply as works of art without any particular ritual significance. They constitute the earliest specimens of stone sculpture produced by the Neolithic Cypriots.

Neolithic II period. Cyprus Museum, Nicosia, no.967. Height: 19 cm.

5

The head of a human figure, from the floor of a
house of Khirokitia. Unlike most of the stone
sculptures from the Neolithic period which are
made of andesite, this is made of unbaked clay
and differs in style considerably from other
Neolithic sculptures, as there is an obvious
attempt on the part of the artist for naturalism.
The eyes and mouth are rendered by grooves,
the nose is in relief. The face is well modelled,
with rounded cheeks and chin. At the back of
the head there are vertical wavy lines in relief,
probably depicting hair, though a suggestion
has been made that the lines may represent
snakes, the symbols of the underworld divinity
which appear often in the Early Bronze Age.

Neolithic I period. Cyprus Museum, Nicosia,
no.1063. Height: 10.5 cm.

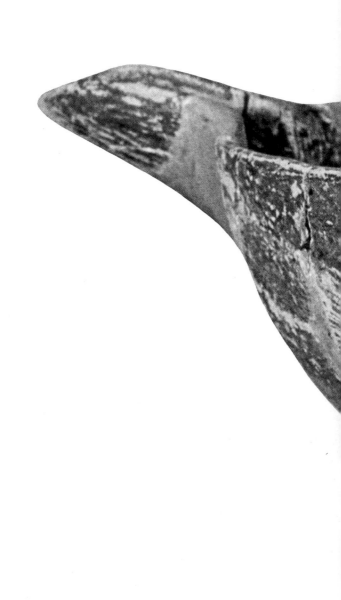

Vessels of baked clay replaced the stone vessels during the Neolithic II period. Apart from bowls there are also closed vessels, mainly bottles with a globular body and a cylindrical neck. The bowls are large, hemispherical, usually with an open spout. The prevailing technique is the so-called 'combed ware'. The surface of the vases (in the case of bowls both inside and out) was covered with a thick slip of brown paint. When the clay was leather-hard, part of the slip was scraped off with a comb-shaped tool so as to uncover the surface of the clay. Thus, the surface of the vase was decorated with wavy bands of 'combed' decoration. This bowl was found at Khirokitia.

Neolithic II period. Cyprus Museum, Nicosia, no.496. Height: 15 cm.; diameter: 32.5 cm.

7

The Chalcolithic period witnessed considerable developments in the art of ceramics. New shapes make their appearance as well as new styles of decoration. The most prevalent among the latter is the so-called 'Red-on-White'. The surface of the vase is applied with a white-creamy slip and on it the decoration is applied in orange to dark brown paint. The decoration consists mainly of long panels which are filled with geometric motifs and occasionally floral patterns. This vase is a large storage jar (*pithos*). Apart from the geometric decoration it is also adorned with curved narrow bands terminating into 'fingers', which are perhaps meant to be human. The artist probably wanted to give an anthropomorphic element to the decoration, a tendency which will develop fully during the Bronze Age.

From Erimi, near the south coast. Chalcolithic period. Cyprus Museum, Nicosia, no.162. Height: 53 cm.; diameter: 38 cm.

8

A composite vase from the Chalcolithic cemetery of Souskiou, near Palaepaphos. It consists of one bottle with a long cylindrical neck and two miniature bottles attached to its body and communicating with it. Composite vases are mainly known from the Early Bronze Age. The decoration, in red paint, is of a geometric character.

Chalcolithic period. Hadjiprodromou Collection, Famagusta, no.968. Height: 13.2 cm.

9

The majority of the vases of the Chalcolithic period known so far were found in the necropolis of Souskiou, where they were placed as tomb gifts to accompany the dead. The exuberant character of the shapes and of the decoration betray a highly-developed artistic taste among Chalcolithic craftsmen. This vase has a false neck and a real neck with spout; the false neck may have served as a handle. This shape may herald the so-called 'stirrup' vases of the Late Bronze Age. The entire body of the vase is decorated with latticed chequers. The base is pointed, like many other vases of the Chalcolithic period, which were probably placed in shallow pits, on benches, or on the earthen floors of the houses.

Chalcolithic period. Pierides Foundation Museum, Larnaca. Height: 17 cm.

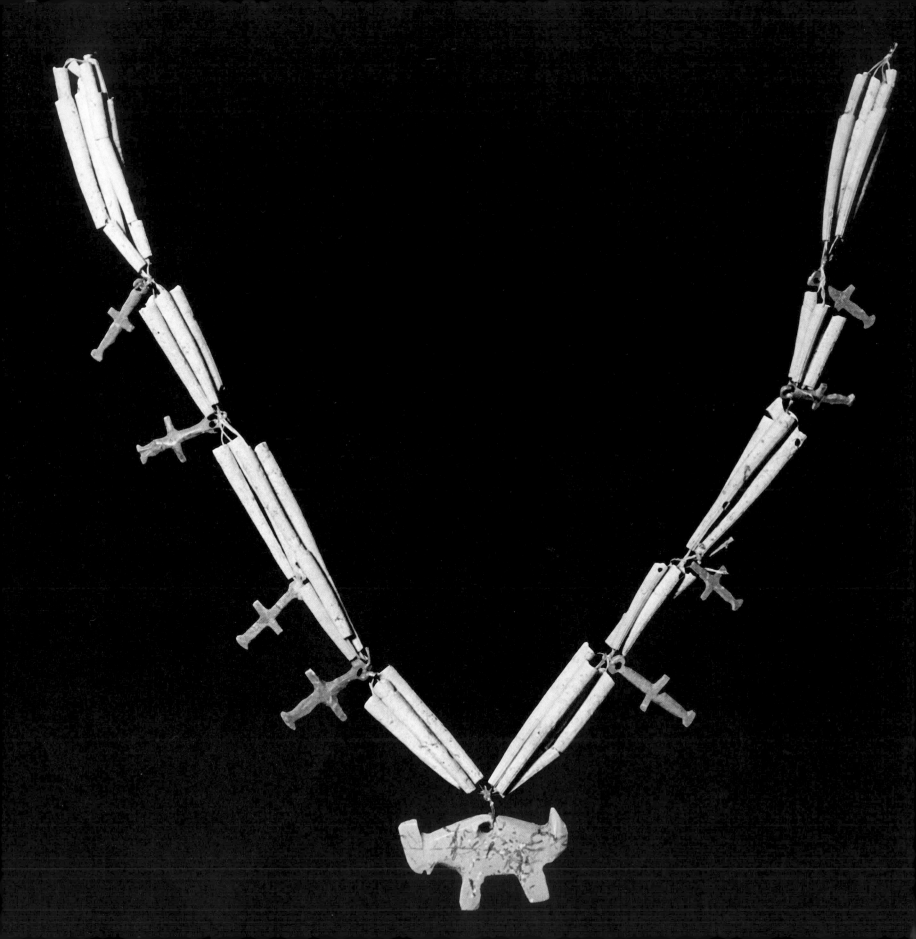

10

The idea of a second life after death was prevalent among the Cypriots from the dawn of the island's prehistory. Apart from utensils and tools offered in tombs as gifts for the dead, there were also ornaments, particularly in the tombs of women. This necklace was found in a tomb of the necropolis of Souskiou. It consists of groups of dentalia and small cruciform steatite pendants in the form of miniature anthropomorphic idols (see no.12). There is also a larger flat pendant in the shape of a quadruped. As dentalia and pendants were found loose and grouped together, the restoration of the necklace is tentative.

Chalcolithic period. Souskiou Tomb 3, no.6.
Cyprus Museum, Nicosia.
Total length: 35.5 cm.

11

The imaginative spirit of the Chalcolithic artist is manifested by the zoomorphic vase shown here, which was found in a tomb of the Chalcolithic necropolis of Souskiou. It is shaped like a quadruped, with an ovoid body and a pointed tail, and is supported on four small legs; it has a long cylindrical neck and a human head with a flattened face; the head is open at the top, thus providing a spout for the vase. The facial characteristics are clearly rendered in relief and with depressions. The entire body is decorated with geometric patterns, in the Red-on-White style of pottery. Such 'monsters' have also been found in the Balkan region, and date to the same period. There may have been a remote common origin for both, but there is no evidence for any direct contacts between Cyprus and the Balkans during this period. This monster may be considered the forerunner of the 'centaurs' of the Aegean, which appear at the end of the 2nd millennium B.C.

Chalcolithic period. Hadjiprodromou Collection, Famagusta, no.1380.
Height: 13.5 cm.; length: 22 cm.

12

Steatite, commonly known as soapstone, is found abundantly along the south-western coast of Cyprus. It was widely used during the Chalcolithic period for making both animal and human idols, as well as pendants of various shapes, and occasionally small vases. The most prevalent steatite objects are the cruciform human idols, with flat stretched arms, long necks and legs separated by a vertical groove. The facial characteristics are summarily rendered in relief. This idol was found in the Paphos District, but its exact provenance is not known. It has a 'necklace' round the neck, with a pendant in the form of a cruciform idol, like those of the other Chalcolithic necklace (no.10).

Chalcolithic period. Cyprus Museum, Nicosia, no.1934/III-2/2. Height: 15.3 cm.

13

The idea of fertility was worshipped by the Chalcolithic Cypriots and personified as a naked woman. This divinity formed the basis of prehistoric religion in Cyprus, as it did in many other countries of the Aegean and the Near East. There were cult places where rituals were performed in honour of the fertility goddess. This limestone statuette was found in one such cult place, at the Chalcolithic settlement of Lemba, near the western coast of Cyprus. It is the largest found so far in a legitimate excavation (a second one, found by looters and now in a private collection in France, is slightly larger). It measures 36 cm. and represents a standing naked woman with schematized breasts and well-defined genitals. She has broad hips and short stretched arms, like the steatite cruciform figurines of the same period. The facial characteristics and the long neck also recall the steatite idols (see no.12).

Chalcolithic period. Cyprus Museum, Nicosia. Height: 36 cm.

27

14

The fertility goddess of the Chalcolithic
period is often represented in terracotta, in
the form of a nude woman, with genitals
distinctly represented by deep grooves. The
terracotta figurine illustrated here has for
many years been in the Louvre Museum in
Paris, but has only recently been correctly
identified and dated. Its facial characteristics
are almost identical with those of legitimately
excavated terracottas from the Chalcolithic
settlement of Erimi. The figurine is nude,
seated, and is shown in the act of pressing
her tattooed breasts for milk to pour in the
basin which is placed on her lap. This must
have been a ritual act of fertility.

Chalcolithic period. Musée du Louvre, Paris,
no.AM 1176. Height: 12.9 cm.

15

Seated figure. The largest terracotta figure
from the Chalcolithic period found so far is
this nude male figure seated on a four-legged
stool, which is probably from Souskiou and is
now in a private collection. The figure is
hollow with a large perforation at the top of
the head. The mouth is open and the teeth
show. The eyes are swollen and have a
depression in the centre. The legs are bent,
with both feet resting on the flat part of the
stool. Both arms are bent upwards, elbows
on the knees, with the hands on either side
of the head below the ears. The tubular penis
is erect. Such figures have been found in the
Balkans, and one very similar but much
smaller figure is known in archaeological
literature as 'The Thinker'.

Chalcolithic period. Pierides Foundation
Museum, Larnaca. Height: 36 cm.

III. THE EARLY BRONZE AGE: A PERIOD OF CONFIDENCE

The Chalcolithic period ends, at Erimi, soon after 3000 B.C. At Lemba (Lakkous), it lingers into the 3rd millennium to a time when the Bronze Age had already been introduced in the north-western part of the island.

In the Ovgos Valley, in the north-western part of Cyprus, a new culture appears, probably the result of an influx from south-western and south Anatolia. The arrival of these peoples to Cyprus coincides with the destruction of the Early Bronze Age II Anatolian culture in c. 3000 B.C., so they may have come to Cyprus as refugees. The first traces of this new culture were found in the village of Philia ("Vasiliko"), west of Nicosia, where four tombs were excavated in 1942. Since then, however, other sites containing pottery from this new "Philia culture", as it is usually known, have been found in a number of places along the Ovgos river (Kyra, Chrysiliou, Ambelikou). Other sites are at Vasilia, west of Kyrenia, near the north coast, and at Dhenia and Ayia Paraskevi, in the central part of Cyprus, near Nicosia. The newcomers appear to have gradually spread inland, and we have found evidence of them even in the southern part of the island, at Anoyira and Sotira. They may have crossed the Troodos Mountains via a natural gorge known as the Amiandos Pass, but there is also a possibility that some of them may have entered Cyprus from the south.

The dominating pottery of the new culture is called "Red Polished ware". The vases (jugs with flat bases and long cutaway necks, two-handled jars, bottles, and so on) are occasionally decorated with engraved zigzags and parallel chevron patterns. Black-Slip-and-Combed ware is represented by small bowls with black slips and red undercoats. Before baking, the potter used a comb-shaped tool to remove some of the black slip, uncovering in the process the red undercoat in parallel bands which recall the Neolithic II "Combed ware". This pottery has also been found at Tarsus in Cilicia, and may lend support to the suggestion that the new settlers were of Anatolian origin.

A recent study of material which came from a stratigraphic excavation carried out in 1942 at Ambelikeu ("Ayios Georghios") near the north-western coast, has demonstrated that the new pottery existed side by side with the late Chalcolithic pottery found in the lower layers of the habitation site. This suggests that there was a peaceful co-existence between the new Bronze Age settlers and the old Chalcolithic Cypriot stock.

The real innovation wrought by the new culture was not its splendid pottery, but in its clever use of a new metal. Bronze adzes, knives, pins and ear-rings have been found in the Philia tombs. At Vasilia large chamber tombs have been found, with funerary gifts that include Philia pottery, bronze daggers, torques, and alabaster bowls and jugs, the latter obviously imported from Egypt.

It has been suggested that the metal weapons found in the tombs of Vasilia and also those of the tombs of Ayia Paraskevi may date to a slightly advanced stage of Early Bronze Age I —a time when a peaceful symbiosis between the newcomers and the local population had been established. The reason for such co-existence may have been that both parties were united in the defence of their main source of wealth— the copper mines in the western region of the island and on the north slopes of the Troodos mountains —against any encroachment by the inhabitants of eastern Cyprus, who lacked copper.

The antagonism between the "industrial" West and the copper-poor agricultural East is a common feature of Cypriot life during the Bronze Age. In fact, the Bronze Age did not make itself felt in the eastern part of Cyprus during Early Bronze Age I or II periods. It was only during the period called Early Bronze Age III, toward the end of the third millennium (c. 2250/2150 B.C.), that the Bronze Age culture spread throughout the island.

There are well-excavated Neolithic and Chalcolithic period settlement sites where one may study not only the chronological sequence of the settlements, but also their architectural styles and everyday patterns of life. But our knowledge of the whole of the Early Bronze Age period is derived entirely from tombs, and thus is limited to objects which while illustrating the art of the period, are of very limited use as tools for studying the everyday life of the period.

The most extensively excavated Early Bronze Age cemetery is at Vounous, on the northern part of the island. Dated to the middle and late phases of the Early Bronze Age (periods II and III; the Philia cultural stage is reckoned as period I), the tombs consist of chambers with short sloping passages (*dromos*), in front of the entrances. The tombs are smaller than those at Vasilia, but they constitute a great advancement in funerary architecture, especially when compared with the pit graves at Ayia Paraskevi, or the irregularly-shaped chambers at Philia. They are rock-cut and their chambers provide ample space for the skeleton and the large number of tomb-gifts (vases, weapons, jewellery, tools, food) which were offered in honour of the dead.

At first, these chambers were used for one or two burials, but gradually they developed into family tombs for multiple burials. The pottery found in them is a development from the Red Polished pottery of Early Bronze Age I. Though the basic material remains the same, one now has a richer variety of forms and decoration. Bowls are decorated with figures-in-the-round like birds, quadrupeds or animal protomes. Common shapes, such as bowls standing on high cylindrical stems and decorated with animal figures or miniature vases around the rim, have been labelled "ritual vases". But this may be due to our inability to understand the spirit of the creative potter who realised suddenly that there were no limits to his craft and that once he had grasped the technique of pottery-making, he could produce wonderful and unusual forms to impress his clientele.

The simple engraved motifs of the Early Bronze Age I have now become complicated patterns, but they still remain abstract and mainly linear. They appear alongside vases with decorations in relief, consisting of motifs like snakes and bulls' heads. Cypriot artists expanded their vision by inventing, perhaps by accident, a technique by which they produced two colours on the surface of their bowls: black inside and outside around the rim, and red on the rest of the surface. This colour scheme was achieved by special firing methods.

The last phase of the Early Bronze Age, dating from c.2250/2150 to c.1900/1800 B.C. is the best known, but, unfortunately, again only from tombs. A house excavated at Alambra that consists of two four-sided rooms in an L-shaped arrangement with a pen for animals within an enclosure, may tell us something about the architectural style of this period, which is considerably developed compared to the primitive Chalcolithic houses. But this is only an isolated case, and the information which it offers is very insufficient. The increase of population as a result of economic growth is apparent; there are more settlements in the vicinity of copper-mining areas, though agriculture continues to be the basis of the economy. A clay model of a ploughing scene found in a tomb at Vounous shows the use of the wooden elbow plough, probably — reflecting the ubiquity of copper — with a metallic ploughshare.

For the first time there is tangible evidence of contact with the outside world. A Syrian jug was found in a tomb of Vounous, dating to the Early Cypriot II period. Now we have unearthed a jar from Crete and faience beads from Egypt. How did these artefacts come to Cyprus? It is not clear whether the island exported perishable goods in exchange, or simply copper. There are, however, tin-bronze implements at Vounous, a fact which presupposes the importation of tin from abroad, probably from Mesopotamia or Anatolia. Actual metallurgical installations of a slightly later period have been found at Ambelikou, near the copper mines. The bronze objects found only in the tombs are now plentiful and are of a variety of types. There are weapons, tools, ornaments, tweezers and razors. On the other hand, objects associated with daily life have been found in abundance in tombs: bronze toggle-pins, silver and gold hair ornaments which were used to hold together locks of hair; beads of faience for necklaces; and spindle whorls. There are also scenes of everyday life with figures depicted in the round on vases: women grinding corn, making bread, pouring liquids and riding animals.

Red Polished ware vases are predominant in the ceramic production with regional variations in the form and decoration. The decoration, incised or in relief, is rich and imaginative. Some of the composite vases are more than 50 cm. tall. They do not, as a rule, serve any practical purpose, but were made by potters who wanted to please rich and demanding clients with unusual objects that could be offered as gifts to the dead.

The sense of humour —and ingenious use— is never lacking in the ceramic production. For example, composite bowls often have high plank-shaped handles terminating at the top into a human figure holding an infant. The figure is perforated with large holes, producing a shape that recalls the style of modern sculptor Henry Moore. There are also askoi, zoomorphic and bird-shaped vases.

The phenomena of life and death impressed prehistoric peoples and formed the basis of religion during the later part of the Early Bronze Age. We found evidence of early religious practices in a clay model of a sanctuary unearthed at Vounous. The model is circular, and depicts a group of people in various attitudes taking part in what seems to be a ritual in honour of three divinities represented in relief against the wall. These plank-shaped idols (xoana) are topped by bulls' heads; snakes hang from their outstretched arms.

The bull and the snakes are symbols of the divinities of fertility and death respectively. A human figure is kneeling in prayer in front of this triad; another one, with a crown on his head, the chief of the community, is seated on a throne.

Others sit on benches and some are standing in a circle. A human figure holding an infant tends oxen that are no doubt meant to be sacrificed. Finally, a human figure climbs up the wall to the sanctuary, to watch what is going on inside —an indication that the ceremony may have been restricted to those who were initiated in some kind of mystic rite.

Apart from the obvious significance this object has in the history of prehistoric religion, it also has great artistic value. Fabricating such a complex scene required considerable skill and imagination, and may be compared with similar scenes from Egypt. Two other clay models of sanctuaries, found in tombs at Kotchati, in the central part of the island, may be abbreviated versions of the Vounous model. Three plank-shaped idols shown in relief against a wall are wearing bull's heads. On the "floor" there is a human figure in front of a large jar, obviously ready to pour libations in honour of the divinity symbolised by the bull. Groups of human figures appearing around the rim of large bowls are often connected with fertility. These include male and female couples. The women are either pregnant, or are seated females with tattooed breasts and hold infants.

The culture of Cyprus during the latter part of the Early Bronze Age developed in a homogeneous manner. The wealth the Cypriots acquired as a result of the exploitation of the copper mines produced new possibilities for the improvement of the quality of everyday life. This, along with the acquisition of new technological skills, gave the Cypriots confidence and a spirit of exaltation that is reflected in their exuberant art.

16, 17

The earliest phase of the Early Bronze Age is characterised by the appearance of Red Polished pottery of a style which is usually known as pottery of the 'Philia culture', after the name of the village in north-western Cyprus where this pottery was found for the first time. Now, however, this pottery is also known in the central and even the southern parts of the island. It comprises mainly jugs with flat bases, long necks and elegant, long, beak-shaped or cut-away spouts. Such jugs are closely parallelled by Anatolian forms and it is believed that this particular shape was first introduced to Cyprus from Anatolia by settlers who came to the island during the first half of the 3rd millennium B.C. They have a red polished surface, occasionally decorated with linear engraved patterns (no.16). An example of Red Burnished ware (no.17) is shown at right.

Jug no.16 was found in a tomb of the necropolis of Philia site Vassiliko (Tomb 1, no.10). Cyprus Museum, Nicosia. Height: 49 cm.
Juglet no.17 was found at the same site (Tomb 1, no.30). Cyprus Museum, Nicosia. Height: 13.5 cm.

18

The full development of Red Polished ware
took place during the mature period of the
Early Bronze Age. Large quantities of vases
from this period (the second half of the 3rd
millennium B.C.) have been found in the
necropolis of Vounous, near Cyprus' northern
coast. The repertory of shapes is enriched and
no longer depends on Anatolian prototypes,
as the Cypriot potter.invented new shapes
which demonstrate a creative and inventive
spirit. The technique is the same (red polished
surface with incised decoration), but there are
now other decorative elements, such as relief
ornaments or figures and miniature vases,
placed as accessories on the shoulder or rim
of vases. This large stemmed bowl is
decorated round the rim with three
quadrupeds, including a fallow deer, and
three miniature bowls. Such vases are usually
labelled as ritual vessels, but in all probability
they are the creations of a potter who wanted
to produce extraordinary shapes in order to
impress his clients.

Early Bronze Age II period. Vounous Tomb
160, no.17. Cyprus Museum, Nicosia.
Height: 52.9 cm.; diameter: 34.9 cm.

19

A deep bowl from the necropolis of Vounous. It belongs to a class which is characterised by a decoration in two colours, red and black polished. By covering the rim and the inside with ashes (placed upside down in the kiln) the pottery was given a black colour, the covered surface not being fully oxidized. The handle of this bowl is in the form of a handle of a dagger. Its rim is decorated with two pairs of protomes of horned animals (three bulls and one ram), two spoon-like projections and a stylised bird. The outside surface of the vase as well as the accessories round the rim are decorated with incisions.

Early Bronze Age II period. From Vounous, Tomb 160, Chamber B, no.12.
Cyprus Museum, Nicosia.
Height: 18.2 cm.; diameter: 17 cm.

20

The vases decorated in the Red and Black polished technique are usually bowls; the technique is rarely seen in jugs. The largest part of this jug is black polished and only the lowest part near the base is red polished. The upper half of the body and the long neck are decorated with incised linear motifs, mainly horizontal bands of zigzag parallel lines. These were intentionally filled with white lime to give prominence to the incised decoration.

Early Bronze Age II period. From Vounous, Tomb 164B, no.24. Cyprus Museum, Nicosia. Height: 43.7 cm.

21

The end of the Early Bronze Age is marked by an exuberant development of the Red Polished pottery. Fancy shapes of vases, mainly with composite bodies or necks, made their appearance. They are not objects to be used in a kitchen, but works of art to offer as gifts to the dead. This jug has a globular body with three long narrow necks; there is only one handle, from between two of the necks to the shoulder, and a long tubular spout on the shoulder opposite the handle. The whole of the surface is decorated with engraved linear patterns.

Early Bronze Age III period. Provenance uncertain. Cyprus Museum, Nicosia, no.1933/I-31/1. Height: 30 cm.

22

The desire of the potter at the end of the Early Bronze Age for originality very often led to excesses, such as this jug. It consists of two superimposed jugs, whose chambers are connected. They each have their own neck and handle, the shoulder of each is decorated with a plastically rendered bird, and there is a third bird on top of the handle of the larger jug. The whole surface is decorated with engraved patterns, mainly groups of concentric segments and parallel zigzag lines.

Early Bronze Age III period. Provenance uncertain. Cyprus Museum, Nicosia, no.1933/VI-7/7. Height: 26 cm.

23

The inventive spirit and the skill of the potters at the end of the Early Bronze Age are perfectly demonstrated by this composite vase. The elegant and graceful vase is of Red Polished ware and consists of four hemispherical bowls supported on a long slender stem, which has a base in the form of three spreading toes.

Early Bronze Age III period. Collection of Dr. Desmond Morris, Oxford. Height: 14 cm.

24
The idea of fertility, which formed the basis of the religious beliefs of the Chalcolithic Cypriots, continued to impress the Cypriots of the Early Bronze Age. This boat-shaped bowl with a lid (*pyxis*) is decorated with standing human figures; a male, and a female holding an infant. The body and lid of the bowl as well as the human figures are decorated with incised patterns.

Early Bronze Age III period. From Vounous Tomb 2, no.91. Cyprus Museum, Nicosia. Length: 22 cm.; height: 19 cm.

25

This vase is an ingenious combination of a composite vase and a figurine. The vase forms the base of the terracotta and the figurine serves as the handle. The vase itself is composite, consisting of four hemispherical bowls. The figurine differs considerably from the other plank-shaped figures (see nos.33,34). Its body has three large perforations. The figure is distinctly female, with breasts, and holds an infant in its arms. It has a long neck and a small head. The perforations through the body and the long body and neck, combined with a small head, are similar to those found in modern sculpture. The red polished surface of the terracotta figure is decorated with engraved patterns. There are necklaces round the neck; the ears are perforated for ear-rings.

Early Bronze Age III period. From Vounous, Tomb 48, no.2. Cyprus Museum, Nicosia. Height: 46 cm. (The bowls are restored).

26

Large jar of Red Polished ware. The vase has a horizontal handle on the shoulder and a long tubular spout opposite and may have been used for milking sheep and goats. The shoulder on either side is decorated with a stemmed goblet, flanked on either side by birds, resting on a cylindrical stem. The bird is often used as a decorative element during this period; it may be associated with the divinity of fertility, just as the dove in later periods became sacred to Aphrodite.

Early Bronze Age III or Middle Bronze Age I period. Perhaps from the necropolis of Kotchati, south of Nicosia. Pierides Foundation Museum, Larnaca. Height: 40 cm.

41

27

Large bowl of Red Polished ware, with twin spouts, a vertical loop handle from rim to body and a round base. The shoulder on either side of the vase is decorated with plastically rendered human figures which are attached to the walls of the vase, some as if in high relief. Some of them are standing and turn towards the rim of the vase; they are perhaps engaged in grinding corn. Others are seated. This is a frequent style in the decoration of large bowls found in tombs. Perhaps the idea was to offer to the dead human figures which would be of service in the afterlife; a primary service would be in the preparation of food.

Early Bronze Age III or Middle Bronze Age I period. Perhaps from the cemetery of Marghi, south of Nicosia. Hadjiprodromou Collection, Famagusta, no.682.
Height: 38 cm.; Diameter: 38 cm.

28

Terracotta figure of Red Polished ware, originally part of the decoration of a large bowl (see no.27). It represents a seated female figure holding an infant. Her breasts are naked and tattooed (see no.14). Though the head betrays the style of the plank-shaped idols (see no.25), the rest of the body is naturalistic.

Early Bronze Age III or Middle Bronze Age I period. Provenance uncertain. Cyprus Museum, Nicosia, no.1970/VI-26/6.
Height: 12.2 cm.

29

Pair of gold hair-rings, perhaps used to decorate women's locks. Such objects are also known in silver and bronze. This pair consists of a triangular thin sheet of gold, decorated in *repoussé* with vertical rows of dots and vertical zigzags. At its base each triangle has a long thin projection. The sheet was rolled to produce a tube, which was held together by the thin projection which was also coiled round the tube. The rings were found on either side of the skull of a woman and are the earliest gold ornaments so far found in Cyprus.

End of the Early Bronze Age III period. From a tomb at Lapithos, near the northern coast. Cyprus Museum, Nicosia. Length: 5.5 cm.

Clay models of scenes from everyday life are of extreme importance to our knowledge of the Early and Middle Bronze Ages, since such material as we have comes mainly from tombs and not from settlements. This clay model was found in a tomb in the cemetery of Vounous. It represents a 'table', supported on five legs, on which there are two pairs of oxen drawing a plough and four other figures, two behind the ploughs and two holding a trough with grain. Cultivating the earth to produce food was at a very advanced stage in prehistoric culture and has been one of the main occupations of the Cypriots since the Neolithic period. Such models, depicting scenes from everyday life, are also known from Egypt.

The very end of the Early Bronze Age III period. From the cemetery of Vounous. Cyprus Museum, Nicosia, special series 1. Length: 41 cm.; height: 19 cm.

31

Clay model of a sanctuary, found in a tomb in the Vounous cemetery. It may represent in miniature an existing sanctuary in the settlement of Vounous which has not yet been excavated. It is in the form of a bowl with a large flat base and a door on the side and must have been an open-air sanctuary. On the wall opposite the door there are three figures in relief, holding snakes (represented by vertical wavy lines) and wearing bulls' masks; we know that the bull and the snake represented the divinities of fertility and death respectively. One human figure kneels in prayer in front of these sacred figures which were probably of wood and were fastened on the wall. Other figures sit on benches or stand in circles; one, with a crown on his head, is seated on a throne. There is a figure near the doorway holding an infant. There are oxen in pens, obviously for sacrifice. A human figure climbs up the wall near the doorway in an effort to see what is going on inside the sanctuary, an indication that the ritual was probably of a mystic character and only those who were initiated could attend.

The very end of the Early Bronze Age III period. Vounous Tomb 22, no.26.
Cyprus Museum, Nicosia.
Height: 8 cm.; diameter: 37 cm.

32
Clay model of a sanctuary in Red Polished ware, found in a tomb at Kotchati. It consists of a rectangular panel on which there are three vertical poles in relief, joined by horizontal bars and topped by bulls' heads. On either side of the central pole there is a horn, fixed on the wall. On the lower part of the panel there is a rectangular 'floor' with a female human figure rendered in the round, standing in front of a large amphora; she is shown in the act of pouring libations in honour of the divinity of fertility which is symbolised by the bulls' heads. The relationship between this model and the one from Vounous (no.31) is obvious.

The very end of the Early Bronze Age III period.
Cyprus Museum, Nicosia, no.1970/V-28/1. Height: 19 cm.

33
Plank-shaped idol in Red Polished ware. This idol has a rectangular body, wide neck forming one piece with the head, a nose in relief, a depression for the mouth, large ears perforated twice, and large eyes rendered by engraved concentric circles. Hair is indicated by parallel chevrons. The front surface of the idol is decorated with engravings filled with white lime. These include necklaces rendered by curved bands filled with transversal lines. The arms are shown by two oblique grooves on the body. Such clay idols may be miniatures of large wooden sculptures (*xoana*) which were used in sanctuaries. This suggestion may be supported by their flat form and the style of their decoration. Though sex is very rarely shown (some have breasts), the necklaces may suggest female figures.

The very end of the Early Bronze Age III or beginning of the Middle Bronze Age.
Cyprus Museum, Nicosia, no.1963/IV-20/12. Height: 26.2 cm.

34
Plank-shaped idol of Red Polished ware, similar to no.33, perhaps by the same artist. From Vounous(?).

The very end of the Early Bronze Age III or the beginning of the Middle Bronze Age.
Cyprus Museum, Nicosia, no.1933/I-17/1. Height: 28 cm.

IV. THE MIDDLE BRONZE AGE: A PERIOD OF UNCERTAINTY

The stability of the Early Bronze Age could not last forever. Antagonism between eastern and western parts of the island, strong in the previous period, sharpened considerably in the Middle Bronze Age. Additionally, a burgeoning population added its own considerable pressure.

The Middle Bronze Age is a relatively short period. Its early years are marked by a peaceful development from the Early Bronze Age III, while its later years are a preparatory period for the cosmopolitanism of the Late Bronze Age. Chronologically one may assign 300 years to this period (Middle Cypriot I-III, c. 1900/1800-1600/1550 B.C.). The chronological criteria for the terminal dates are provided by Minoan imports to Cyprus at the very beginning of the Middle Bronze Age and by Cypriot objects found in Egypt and Palestine at the start of the Late Bronze Age.

Unlike the Early Bronze Age, whose documentation is limited to finds in tombs, the Middle Bronze Age presents several settlements with adjoining cemeteries. Some of these settlements are currently being excavated or have been excavated very recently. Such sites include Kalopsidha in the eastern part of the island; Episkopi ("Phaneromeni"), near the south coast; and Alambra, in the central part. Middle Bronze Age architecture is considerably advanced, and includes houses with a fairly large number of rooms. The four-sided dwellings had flat roofs, and were constructed at the lower part with rubble and at the upper part with mud bricks. At Phaneromeni a house with a second storey has been found, while at Alambra, a recently uncovered house has large rooms (one measures 7.5 × 6 m.) with very thick walls. The house excavated at Kalopsidha in 1924 has 10 rooms. The various rooms served a distinct purpose. Some were store-rooms, kitchens, or workshops.

Evidence for considerable industrial activity has been found on the floors of the houses at Phaneromeni. There were stone troughs, mortars and pestles, etc. Though none of the settlements has been extensively excavated, we have found, at Kalopsidha and Phaneromeni, traces of streets running along one side of the houses. Perhaps one day, when larger spaces are uncovered, a picture of Middle Cypriot town planning will emerge for the first time.

Apart from domestic architecture, there is now substantial evidence of "military" architecture, no doubt a result of the increasing wealth and power of the inhabitants. The pattern of settlement changed considerably compared with that of the Early Bronze Age. The Vounous necropolis gradually declined and Lapithos, on the north coast, became extremely important, and probably controlled most of the export trade in copper from the rich mining area on the north slopes of the Troodos mountains. The "capital" site at the eastern part of Cyprus was Kalopsidha. More settlements were established along the northern fringe of the Mesaoria plain and also in the Karpass peninsula, an area that was deserted in the Early Bronze Age.

In almost all these regions the population was under the continuous threat of attack from locals, or from inhabitants on either of the two antagonistic parts of the island. Fortresses or refuges were built at Krini and Dhikomo, on the south slope of the Kyrenia mountains; at Nikolidhes and Ayios Sozomenos, in the central part of Cyprus; and at Nitovikla, in the Karpass peninsula. The location of these fortresses, away from or isolated from the sea, is indicative of the fact that they were not built to defend the island against invaders. The later part of the period coincides with the raids of the Hyksos, though there is no evidence that these Asiatic tribes ever set foot on Cyprus. Nor is there any evidence of any actual war: the large numbers of skeletons in tombs along the northern part of Cyprus, south of the Kyrenia mountains, may have been the result of an epidemic.

Funerary architecture follows the traditional rock-cut chamber tombs of the Early Bronze Age, with a short *dromos*. But later on there are several innovations, as for instance the long narrow stepped *dromos*, and the low *tumulus* (an earthen mound) above the tombs at Palaeoskoutella in the Karpass, which was obviously influenced by tombs in the Near East. At Karmi, on one of the side walls of the *dromos* of a tomb is a crude, carved human figure. This is the earliest funerary relief known on Cyprus, and was probably influenced by Egyptian funerary art.

The island was prosperous, if one can judge from the wealth of the gifts found in tombs like those at Lapithos. Farming must have been the main occupation of the inhabitants, but settlements near the mining areas grew in numbers and importance and tin-bronze implements were produced in workshops like those at Ambelikou. Metallurgy was a growing skill that was destined to become the major source of Cyprus' wealth during the Late Bronze Age.

Trade in copper was a major occupation of part of the population, and continued to be so until iron replaced bronze as a hard metal. A clay model of a ship, now in the Louvre, may illustrate a scene in a Cypriot harbour where copper was shipped abroad. Kalopsidha pursued commercial relations with the Levant through the harbour at Enkomi. The south coast may have had its own harbour near Episkopi-Phaneromeni. Previously believed to have been deserted during the Middle Bronze Age, a recent surface survey now shows that the area was densely populated during this period. That Cyprus was widely known for its copper is indicated in the tablets of Alalakh and Mari in Mesopotamia from the 18th and 17th centuries B.C. respectively, which name "Alashiya" (Cyprus) as a copper-producing country. The metal must have been exchanged for tin, perhaps in Anatolia or Mesopotamia, for the production of tin-bronze. With a growing industry and commerce new means of transport were introduced, namely the horse and the donkey. The horse may have come from north Syria. Skeletons have been found in excavations.

The regionalism and division rampant in various parts of the island find their illustration in the numerous experimental ceramic styles that were produced during this period. Though Red Polished ware continued to be produced in a rather debased form, the White Painted ware dominated. In this type of ware, the surface of the vases is white and the decoration is applied with a brownish red or black colour. At the beginning this white-painted pottery is elegant (White Painted II), but later on it develops into a pompous style. Vases are overloaded with all kinds of geometric patterns which fill rectangular panels or horizontal zones round the body of the vases. Pottery forms are equally overloaded with accessories and perforated lugs. There is an attempt to give an anthropomorphic appearance to vases by adding faces, breasts and even arms. The eastern part of the island produced its own regional vase type: Red-on-Black, which consists of a predominantly linear decoration in black paint over a red surface. In the Lapithos area the White Painted and geometric pattern style was predominant.

Among the many forms in the ceramic repertory of this period, of particular note are the zoomorphic and bird-shaped *askoi,* and terracotta figures, both human and animal. The human figures are often plank-shaped, but unlike earlier figures, a serious attempt was made to render facial characteristics correctly (one figure has a long beard and large perforated ears; another has a grotesque face). The arms and legs are distinctly shown, rather than implied, as is the case with earlier plank-shaped idols.

Terracotta female figures holding infants or groups of male and female figures have been found in tombs, and perhaps served as female "companions" to the male. We have also found terracotta groups of women preparing food or grinding corn, obviously for the benefit of the dead in a second life.

The diversity of this period was made possible by the export of copper to the countries of the Syro-Palestinian coast from places like Enkomi and Hala Sultan Tekké (both of which were small harbour townships at the end of the Middle Cypriot III period). Though antagonisms continued between the eastern and western parts of Cyprus, there were increasing commercial exchanges between the two regions, a fact that resulted in the flattening of regional differences and laid the groundwork for the homogeneous culture realised during the next period.

35

A boat-shaped pyxis of White Painted ware, from the cemetery of Vounous. On the shoulder of the pyxis at the end of each of the long sides there is a protome of a horse and a rider. These are decorative accessories, a fashion which was common in the ceramic styles of this period, but at the same time are tangible evidence for the introduction of the horse to the island during this period. On either side of the mouth of the pyxis there are two horizontal raised loop handles.

Beginning of the Middle Bronze Age. Vounous Tomb 64, no.138. Cyprus Museum, Nicosia. Height: 23.5 cm.; length: 39.5 cm.

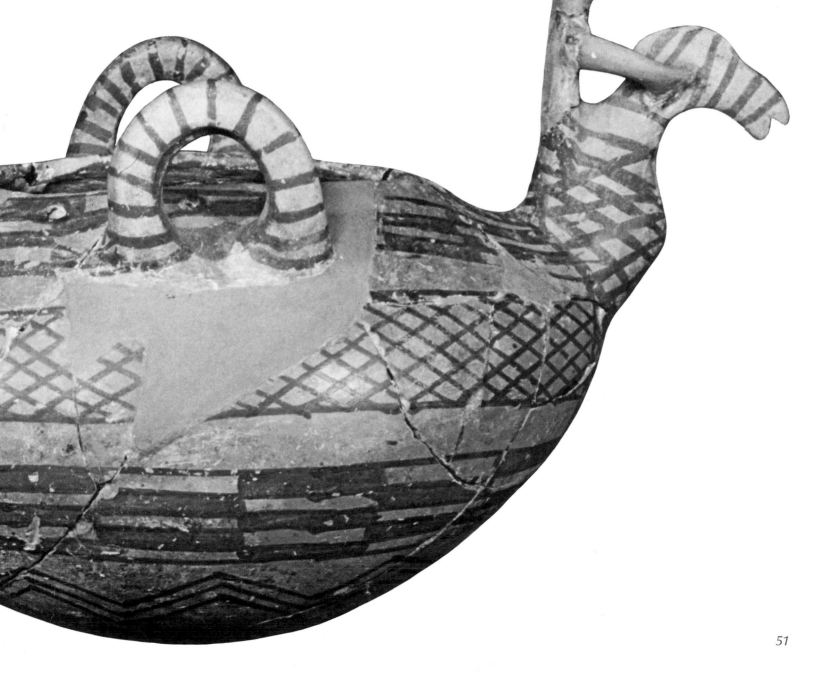

36

The elegance of the Early Bronze Age Red Polished ware was lost during the Middle Bronze Age, which is characterised by a constant search for innovation and new styles by potters. A common trend was to attribute anthropomorphic features to the body or neck or mouth of the vase to make it look like a human being. This vase is a composite one, of White Painted ware, decorated with string-hole projections. At the top of the neck there are two ears and a nose and on the shoulder short arms. The two jugs are united, as if they represented a couple. The surface is decorated with geometric patterns.

Middle of the Middle Bronze Age period. Uncertain provenance. Pierides Foundation Museum, Larnaca. Height: 29 cm.

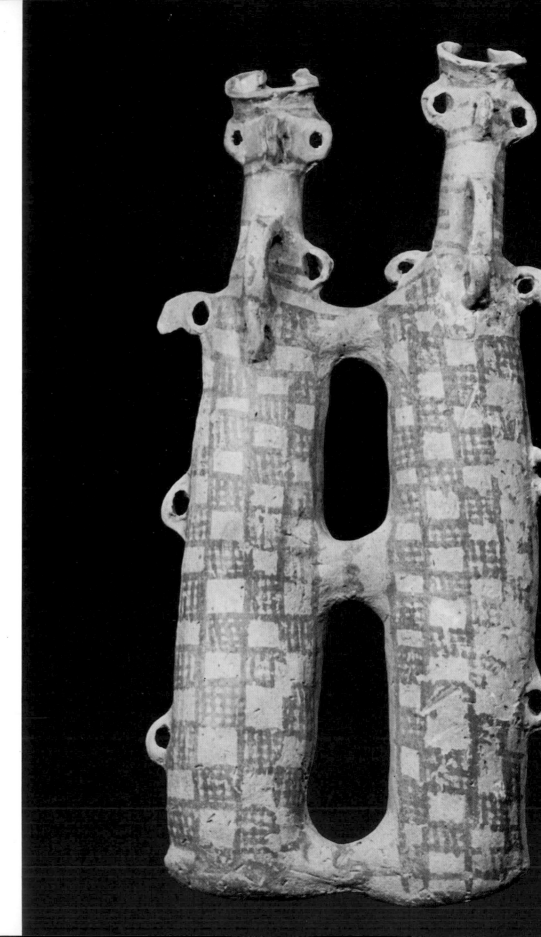

37

A jug of White Painted ware, but painted with black and purple decorations, perhaps in imitation of the Bichrome Wheelmade ware (see no.40). The upper part of the neck is moulded in the shape of a human head, of which the facial characteristics are rendered with black and purple paint. On the shoulder, on either side of the handle, there are two short projections, probably indicating arms; thus the whole vase may be taken as a human figure. The body is decorated with linear geometric patterns.

End of the Middle Bronze Age. From Morphou, near the northern coast. Hadjiprodromou Private Collection, Famagusta, no.579. Height: 23.5 cm.

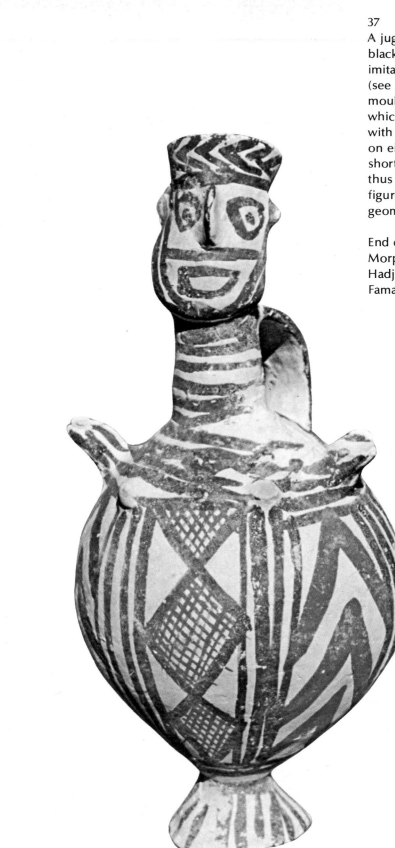

38

Clay model of a ship with a crew of eight arranged round the rim, together with two birds. The surface of the boat and the human figures are decorated in the White Painted style with linear patterns. The human figures are represented in lively attitudes, making gestures with their arms. This is one of the earliest representations of a boat found in Cyprus and clearly illustrates life in the busy harbour towns of the island at a time when trade with the outside world was well developed.

Middle of the Middle Bronze Age. Uncertain provenance. Musée du Louvre, Paris, no.AM 972. Height: 17 cm.; length: 25 cm.; width: 7 cm.

39
Terracotta group in Red Polished ware, probably detached from the shoulder of a large bowl (see no.27). It consists of seven human figures standing in front of an oblong trough. Five are engaged in grinding or washing, one holds an infant and another a vase. They all have headdresses and wear two or three rows of necklaces, which are shown in relief; most prominent is the figure holding an infant, who has pierced ears. The mouth and eyes are rendered by depressions and the nose is in relief.

Middle Bronze Age. Musée du Louvre, Paris, no.AM 816. Height: 13 cm.; length: 27.7 cm.; depth: 12.5 cm.

V. THE LATE BRONZE AGE: A PERIOD OF COSMOPOLITANISM

The Late Bronze Age period in Cyprus (c. 1600/1550 B.C.) is also known as "Late Cypriot" period. The first decades of the Late Bronze Age differ little from the period of tension and anxiety that marked the closing years of the Middle Bronze Age. Some of the old fortresses were destroyed and rebuilt and new ones were constructed, like the one at Enkomi on the east coast. It is doubtful, though not impossible, that raids by the Hyksos spurred the construction or reconstruction of any of these fortresses. But when the Hyksos were expelled from Egypt and the XVIIIth Dynasty was established, a new era of peace and prosperity began in the Eastern Mediterranean.

The Egyptians kept the peace in the region (records of Thutmose III indicate Cyprus, or *Asi* as it was called by the Egyptians, was annexed by Egypt). As a result, Cyprus developed trade both with the Near East and the Aegean. The two traditional antagonists, the peoples living in the eastern and western parts of Cyprus, settled their differences. The island as a whole was on the road to prosperity and homogeneous cultural development. Given a chance to develop peacefully, the coastal towns gained in importance as harbours from which international trade was conducted. The agricultural hinterland grew, as did the industrial centres in the mining areas, where at least part of the smelting of copper ore took place. In the north-western part of Cyprus, the new harbour towns, Toumba tou Skourou and Ayia Irini, asserted their influence. But the major centres continued to be Enkomi on the east coast and Hala Sultan Tekké and Maroni on the south coast.

During the latter part of the Late Bronze Age (c. 1300 B.C.), a chain of new harbour towns sprang up along Cyprus' south coast. Since copper was exported from the coast, there must have been some sort of agreement among the various harbour towns for free passage of this metal, as well as an arrangement for sharing in the supply of copper ore extracted from distant mining areas. Despite such cooperation, it is probable that the various harbour towns were politically and economically independent of one another. Did they all recognise a king who resided in the most important of these towns, Alashiya, which gave also its name to the whole island? No one knows, though perhaps one day the deciphering of the inscribed clay tablets from Enkomi will clarify this mystery.

Very few architectural remains date to the beginning of the Late Bronze Age. This is because building continued unabated in the same areas down to the end of the Late Bronze Age, altering and in some cases obliterating earlier efforts. Nonetheless, what is left is impressive. There are monumental remains of a fortress at Enkomi, which consist of a large rectangular building measuring 34 m. in length and 12 m. in width with massive walls. At Morphou-Toumba tou Skourou, some important industrial installations have been found for pottery-making. Kilns, basins for refining clay, benches and large lumps of clay, found on the floors of these workshops, point to a large ceramic industry whose products have been found in tombs excavated in the immediate vicinity of the workshops.

One of these tombs is of particular importance, both for its architecture and its contents. The tomb consists of a circular shaft with 13 niches which were used for infant burials. Below these are three rock-cut chambers for the burial of adults. This was undoubtedly a family tomb and had been in use for about a century, to judge from the three dozen skeletons which were found in it, and from the chronological range of the tomb gifts. Excavators found pieces of gold and silver and objects of ivory —including a plaque with the earliest representation of the Near Eastern goddess Anat engraved on it.

Some of the pottery is of particular interest, as it is of non-Cypriot origin. This is not really too surprising, as Cyprus by this time was a cosmopolitan island and drew traders from around the Mediterranean, including Aegeans. The pottery is artistically striking. It includes a jug of so-called Tell-el-Yahudiya ware. Imported from Egypt, it is decorated with engraved representations of birds and lotus flowers, recalling the Nilotic scenes of Egyptian art. Of special significance are the fragments of 13 or so vases of Cretan manufacture. These fragments are dated to c. 1525-1475 B.C., and suggest contacts between the Mediterranean and Aegean cultures. While relations with Crete had started by the beginning of the Middle Bronze Age, it is unclear whether these relations were direct. The existence of very few Cretan objects from this period in Cyprus and very few Cypriot objects on Crete seem to argue for indirect contacts. Of course it is also possible that only one commodity was exported from Cyprus to Crete: copper.

Commercial relations between Cyprus and the Near East were much closer than those with the Aegean. Nevertheless, at about this time Crete gave Cyprus a linear script, akin to the "Linear A" script of Minoan Crete, which is known as "Cypro-Minoan". Several tablets containing texts in this script have been found at Enkomi, the oldest one dating to c. 1500 B.C. Later on, the script acquired a cuneiform aspect. The texts were engraved in horizontal lines, on cushion-like clay tablets which were later baked, in an Oriental rather than Aegean fashion. In one case a clay cylinder was engraved with more than 200 signs of the script, the only complete long text possessed up to now, as all other clay tablets are fragmentary.

In the Aegean, such script appears only on clay tablets, which were confined to the archives of palaces. But on Cyprus, the script appeared, in the 14th century B.C., on a variety of objects, which means that it was understood not just by a priest caste, but by a broad spectrum of the population. There are three categories of script, found in excavations in the Aegean region, which constitute what are known as Cypro-Minoan 1, 2 and 3 groups. The first group was used throughout the island, on a variety of objects, engraved or painted. There are about 80 signs in this script. Linguists confirm that the language for which it was used was uniform throughout Cyprus. This group was used until the 11th century B.C.

The second language group appears on inscribed clay tablets found at Enkomi. At least one of these tablets, the restored size of which has been calculated to be 22 × 19 cm., is said to contain a poem or religious text, since some of the lines do not terminate at the end of the column. This script consists of 60 signs and may have been used for a different language than that of Cypro-Minoan 1.

Group 3 appears on clay tablets found at Ugarit in northern Syria. On one of these tablets is a list of proper names, of which the French philologist Madame Masson has been able to recognise 20 out of 25. Several attempts have been made to decipher the script of the tablets, but up to now without success, the basic difficulty being that the language the script represents is not known. Some scholars have suggested that it may be Hurrian, an ancient language of south-eastern Anatolia.

Though there were foreign ethnic elements in Cyprus from the middle of the 2nd millennium B.C. onwards, archaeological evidence does not support the massive presence of Hurrians required for the imposition of the language on a powerful centre like Enkomi. Nor could this language have been some hitherto unknown variant of Greek, since the texts appear long before the Mycenaean colonisation of Cyprus.

Just where did this script originate? If the idea of Cretan parentage is accepted —and some scholars reject this altogether— one faces the problem of the rather meagre evidence for close relations between Cyprus and Crete c. 1500 B.C. For the time being, the only satisfactory explanation may be that the Cypriots and the Cretans met in Ugarit, on the Syrian coast opposite Cyprus, where both had commercial colonies, and that it was here that the Cypriots borrowed the Cretan script and used it for their own language, which still remains unknown to us. Another problem connected with the script is how the language of the tablets continued to be the indigenous Cypriot language, when by the 12th century B.C.

Mycenaean Greek was the language of the Cypriot ruling classes. The explanation that the Mycenaean rulers used local Cypriot scribes is not at all satisfactory. There are, therefore, many enigmas related to the language and the script of Cyprus of the second half of the second millennium which still await solution.

What is more certain is why the Cypriots needed a script in the first place. As urban communities grew along with commercial relations with the outside world, a clear and concise form of communication became essential. Thus, there was an increase in the number of engraved seals, particularly the cylinder seals, which became very common during the 14th and 13th century B.C., when "conoid stamp" seals first appear. These seals were used for the authentification of official documents and for other administrative purposes. Apart from their own functional significance, these seals are also important as works of art. Many of them exhibit an amalgamation of Aegean and Near Eastern elements in their iconography, though the Near Eastern elements are as a rule prevalent. The seals were made of many materials, ranging from the rather commonplace steatite and haematite, to lapis lazuli and paste.

Although relations among the various parts of the island were peaceful, various urban centres still had defensive walls. At Kition, on the south coast, a wall was built at the beginning of the 13th century B.C. It was constructed at the lower part with blocks of stone and at the upper part with mud bricks. There were rectangular towers at regular intervals. Two of these structures have so far been uncovered. One measures 18 by 5 m. and is preserved to a height of 2.50 m. Considering that the northern part of the city wall of Kition followed the perimeter of a low plateau, the edges of which abut on marshes, one may assume that these towers were built right in the marshes.

Large portions of Enkomi on the east coast have been excavated and more is known about domestic architecture there than anywhere else on the island. The houses were usually built around the three sides of a rectangular courtyard. Within the courtyard there are usually family chamber tombs cut into the rock. This feature confused early excavators of the town, who uncovered the tombs but considered the architectural remains all round them to be of a much later date.

Workshops for the smelting of copper were found both at Enkomi and at Kition. At Enkomi they date to the Late Cypriot I period and were built near the northern part of the city wall. At Kition they were at first constructed near the middle of the town, but were later transferred to the northern part, near the city wall, as was the case at Enkomi. The reason for this movement must have been ecological — i.e., so the prevailing southerly winds would blow away the poisonous fumes of the kilns. On the floors of the workshops excavators found the remains of several kilns, fragments of crucibles and bellows and pounders — all mixed with ashes and copper slag.

Funerary architecture follows older traditions: rock-cut chamber tombs with a short *dromos*. But there is also an innovation: *tholoi* built of stone, of which three specimens have been found at Enkomi. In one case there is a superstructure of baked bricks. These dwellings have a more or less circular, rather small chamber, and a short pit *dromos*. Despite the fact that they recall specimens of Aegean funerary architecture, it is not possible that the inspiration came from that region. This is because the earliest of the Enkomi *tholoi* date to soon after 1600 B.C., a time when relations with the Aegean were not sufficiently strong to influence Cypriot funerary architecture. The other *tholoi* date to the 15th and 14th centuries B.C. It is more probable that they were influenced by prototypes from the Near East, perhaps from Megiddo in Palestine. The other novel type of tomb, for Cyprus, is a rectangular chamber with a flat roof and a stepped *dromos* constructed entirely of stone blocks and slabs.

Sacred architecture is also represented in several Late Bronze Age centres. There is a rural sanctuary at Ayios Iakovos, dating to the Late Cypriot II period. It consists of a large fenced circular area, in which there are two altars, perhaps dedicated to two divinities which were worshipped together, probably a mother goddess and her champion. At Kition, there are two sanctuaries at the northernmost part of the town, near the city wall. They are of a purely Near Eastern type, consisting of a narrow holy of holies and an open courtyard, in which there was a hearth altar and a table for offerings. In the courtyard of the largest of the two sanctuaries was a portico along each of the two long parallel walls of the courtyard. The portico roof was supported by wooden pillars. The area between the two sanctuaries at Kition was occupied by a "sacred garden". It contained bushes or flowers and was irrigated by channels which are still visible on the rock of the courtyard. The garden had a boundary wall along its south limit; the north limit was the city wall.

Interestingly enough, art as much as architecture tells one a great deal about a society. Thus, the cultural, and to a certain extent, the political unification of Cyprus resulted in the creation of an art characterised by a homogeneity never before seen on the island, though some regionalisms still persisted. By this time, the ceramists had purified and simplified their art, creating two standard types of pottery that quickly gained dominance over all other types, and were favoured for export to the Near East and the Aegean. One variety is White Slip ware, which consists mainly of bowls with wishbone handles, and jugs and tankards. The vases are covered with a thick smooth white slip, which is decorated with narrow bands filled with linear motifs of orange to dark brown paint. This pottery appears first during the Late Cypriot I period, and by the end of the 13th century B.C., it dies out.

The numerous metal vases which circulated round the island during the Late Bronze Age caused innovative potters to imitate them with vases whose surfaces had metallic qualities.

These vases, usually bowls with raised wishbone handles, or jugs with tall necks and elegant cut-away spouts, have thin walls, and "metallic" decoration like "rope" ornaments in relief. As most of these vessels have ring bases, they are called Base Ring ware. What is interesting is that both White Slip and Base Ring pottery have a primitive appearance and were handmade at a time when potters in neighbouring countries were using the wheel to make pottery. Even on Cyprus itself, a group of foreign potters, probably Syrians, were producing Bichrome pottery, on the wheel. They used geometric and other abstract motifs, but occasionally pictorial motifs, such as birds, fishes, quadrupeds, and even human figures.

The wealth the Cypriots acquired as a result of copper export may be seen in their material culture and particularly in the quantity and quality of objects which accompany the dead as tomb gifts.

Apart from the local Cypriot pottery, there was, from the beginning of the 14th century B.C., an influx of Mycenaean pottery. While some Mycenaean vases were placed in tombs prior to 1400 B.C., by 1400 B.C., their numbers increased considerably. An intriguing question is whether all these vases were made in the Aegean and were exported to Cyprus, or whether some of them could have been made on the island by Mycenaean potters who may have accompanied traders working in the major harbour towns on Cyprus' south and east coasts.

It should be noted that by c. 1400 or slightly later, after what is usually referred to as the "fall of Knossos", the Mycenaeans became masters of the Aegean and replaced the Minoans as major traders with the countries of the Eastern Mediterranean. Cyprus was an ideal place from which to pursue this trade, and was, moreover, attractive because of its wealth of copper. This may be the reason why small *emporia* were established in the main coastal towns.

The Mycenaean pottery found on Cyprus and other Near Eastern sites is so special that several scholars went so far as to call it Cypro-Mycenaean or Levanto-Mycenaean. The large craters (amphoroid or open) were very popular, as the broad zones between their handles offered an ideal space for pictorial compositions, all of them of Aegean character like bulls, octopuses and chariot scenes.

Wealthy Cypriots must have been particularly fond of such fancy, high-quality pottery. Excavators have found numerous vases of this style on Cyprus. Some of these were exported to Ugarit and other Near Eastern centres, where large quantities of Cypriot pottery have also been found.

During the 14th century, the decorative motifs and compositions of the pictorial style recall the major art of fresco painting of the Aegean, in spite of some Levantine peculiarities. This is the so-called Mycenaean IIIA style. Some of the compositions may even be interpreted in terms of Greek mythology, as for example the well-known amphoroid crater from Enkomi which is decorated with octopuses and with a chariot composition. A long-robed human figure holding scales stands in front of the horses. The Swedish scholar Martin Nilsson suggested that this may represent a well-known scene from the *Iliad*, where Zeus is mentioned as holding the "scales of destiny" in front of warriors before they depart for battle.

By the 13th century B.C., the pictorial motifs had become more stylised and were inspired by embroideries and tapestries. This is what is known as the Mycenaean IIIB style. The hands of several individual painters have been recognised by scholars. In most cases all of the vases which have been attributed to the same painter have been found in Cyprus and the Levant. Several forms are peculiar to these regions. These include the lentoid flask; the jug with an angular shoulder and a trefoil mouth; and the handleless chalice. These forms may serve to strengthen the suggestion that some of this pottery could have been made in Cyprus by Mycenaean artists.

Though the problem of the origin of the Mycenaean pictorial style is still unsolved, in spite of attempts to solve it by clay analysis (spectographic or neutron activation), no doubt it constitutes a major artistic contribution to a Late Bronze Age art in whose creation and development Cyprus was directly or indirectly involved.

Pottery is not the only artefact found in tombs during this period. In a 14th century B.C. tomb from Enkomi a silver bowl was found. The bowl is decorated on the outside with rosettes, lotus flowers and a horizontal row of ox heads. All these motifs are inlaid in gold and a black substance called *niello*. This technique is very rare. A similar but less ornate vase was found in the Peloponnese. It is not easy to say whether the Enkomi bowl was made in Cyprus by an Aegean artist or was imported from the Aegean. The Enkomi tombs produced several other exceptional silver bowls, one imitating the form of the well-known cups of Vaphio in the Peloponnese.

The Cypriot market must have attracted not only traders, but foreign craftsmen and artists as well. This is clear from the distinctive style of a number of artefacts. Seals, for example, were carved in the Aegeo-Oriental style. Not only are there Aegean elements in the rendering of motifs, but also in iconography. In jewellery there is a whole class of gold diadems which are decorated in *repoussé* with Cypriot motifs. But occasionally Aegean motifs appear, like the winged sphinxes wearing characteristic flat bonnets, which were found in tombs at Enkomi. Of Aegean inspiration is the lion on the bezel of a gold-plated finger ring found in a tomb at Enkomi. Also Aegean in character are necklaces with gold beads in the form of figure-8 shields.

Typically Cypriot are gold ear-rings shaped like bull's heads, which are mostly embossed, but sometimes have a granulated decoration; ear-rings that are boat-shaped, flat, crescent-shaped, or are fashioned of plated wire; gold toggle-pins, some of them partly made of plated wire; and pendants shaped like pomegranates and decorated with granulated triangles.

Finally, there is a conical vase (*rhyton*) of faience which embodies several different styles. Found in a tomb at Kition, it is decorated on three registers. The upper register contains two galloping bulls and a goat; the middle register, men hunting bulls; and the lower register, vertically arranged "running spirals". In form, the rhyton is Aegean, and so are some of the motifs: e.g. the running spirals. But other motifs, like the bull hunters with kilts and headdress, are Oriental; one of the hunters wears sandals on which appear the Egyptian "magic knives" motif. The decoration is either painted in black and yellow on the thick blue enamelled surface, or is inlaid in red enamel. It is also probable that this vase was imported to Cyprus from Syria or Egypt.

For all the relative leisure afforded the Cypriot craftsmen and their trading partners to produce wondrous artefacts, the relative peace of the Late Bronze Age was still liable to be broken by sudden, violent events that are revealed in tablets. Thus, conditions prevailing in Cyprus and the Eastern Mediterranean in the early 14th century B.C. are reflected in correspondence between the powerful Egyptian Pharaoh Akhenaten and the king of Alashiya, as Cyprus was known in those days. The king of Alashiya calls the Pharoah his "brother" and sends him gifts, mainly ingots of copper, as tribute. "My brother, behold", says the king in a letter dated to the second quarter of the 14th century B.C., "I have sent to thee five hundred [talents] of copper... Let not my brother take it to heart that the copper is little. For in my land the hand of Nergal [the god of war], my lord, has killed all the men of my land, and so there is no one here to produce copper".

The cause for the vassal king's embarrassing situation may have been more temporal: raids by peoples called the Lucci (the Lycians?) from nearby Anatolia, who according to other "letters" often devastated the land of Alashiya.

The Cypriot king also sent the Pharaoh oil, wood, horses and ivory tusks. The latter, of course, were not from Cyprus, but must have come from a stock of such gifts kept in palace workshops. The king, in his turn, asked the Pharaoh to send him gifts which included a bedstead of ebony inlaid with gold, a gold chariot, silver and "good oil".

Other references to Cyprus are made in Hittite tablets, where the island is mentioned as a dependency of the Hittites from c.1400 to 1200 B.C. (This statement cannot be substantiated by archaeological evidence). The Hittite king Shuppiluliuma II is said to have fought a naval battle against Alashiya, during which he devastated the Alashiyan fleet and ordered them to pay tribute to him consisting of silver and copper. Women and children were taken as prisoners to Hattusa, his capital. These events, however, cannot be substantiated by archaeological evidence.

By the end of the Late Cypriot III period (c.1200-1050 B.C.), the sporadic strife that marked the previous period had intensified and the region underwent another, more profound, change. Around the end of the 13th century B.C., Mycenae and Pylos, the major Mycenaean centres in the Peloponese, were abandoned, perhaps as a result of a general disruption of Mycenaean society. The inhabitants sought new lands to settle. They found their way to the island of Rhodes, and thence to Asia Minor, where they raided coastal towns along the Eastern Mediterranean. When they reached Cyprus, they were joined by other adventurers and became what is known (from Egyptian accounts) as the "Sea Peoples". Some of them must have settled in Cyprus, having taken advantage of the weakened population, and others in Palestine, just after 1200 B.C.

Scholars have identified the majority of these warlike peoples with the Achaeans of Homer, since the predominant ethnic element of their material culture, particularly their pottery, was Mycenaean Greek.

Their influence on Cyprus was enormous; in a relatively short period of time, they had colonised the island. But first came a period of struggle. These so-called "Sea Peoples" probably caused the destruction of Cypriot coastal towns like Kition and Enkomi. Certainly there is ample evidence of a great upheaval in these places around the time Mycenaean influence began to be felt.

At Kition the workshops used for copper smelting in the Late Cypriot II period were abandoned and transferred to the northernmost part of the town, near the city wall. The mud brick city wall was destroyed and on its debris a new "cyclopean" city wall was constructed, so-called because it was built at the lower part with two parallel rows of huge stones (the upper part was made of sundried bricks). The ruined houses of the Late Cypriot II period were covered by a thick layer of clayish soil and a new town was built on top. The Late Cypriot II tombs were looted for gold and other metallic objects.

At Enkomi we observed similar phenomena — as well as strong evidence that changes in both towns came about as a result of conquest. Bronze swords of a European type make their appearance for the first time. They are found in association with Aegean bronze greaves and with pottery which is a local imitation of Mycenaean ware. These are mainly shallow bowls decorated with matt-red painted bands on the sides and spirals on the bottoms. Similar pottery was found in a tomb at Kition, which is dated to the time of the destruction of the town. The same tomb also produced deep bowls (skyphoi) in a style which imitated the Achaean pottery of c.1200 B.C. This evidence suggests that the Achaeans responsible for the destruction of Kition and Enkomi must have reached the island in c.1200 B.C. or slightly earlier and that these two towns were restored a few years later, perhaps after the arrival from the Peloponnese of a new wave of Achaean settlers.

The difficulty of pinpointing the initial date of the Achaean colonisation of Cyprus has been greatly lessened by recent excavations at a locality on the west coast, north of Paphos, known as "Maa-Palaeokastro". On a promontory with steep sides, measuring c.300m. in length and c.150m. in maximum width, we have uncovered evidence for one of the earliest Achaean settlements on Cyprus. There is a fortified wall across the "neck" of the promontory, which was used to defend the settlement from land raids, and another wall at the promontory's tip, where the surface of the land slopes down to the sea-shore. This wall was used as a defence against sea-borne raids. There was no need to build a wall along the sides due to the steep cliffs.

Within this small but well-defended area, which was a military outpost for about 300 people, are small houses and other forts. As there are no previous signs of habitation at the site, the fortification can be dated to the arrival of the early Achaeans. The pottery is both local (Base Ring II, White Slip II) as well as "Mycenaean IIIB", dating to the last quarter of the 13th century B.C. (Late Cypriot IIC).

There is no doubt that the settlers were Achaeans, especially if one compares their fortifications and the pottery in houses there to similar structures and pottery found at Enkomi and Kition. The houses have only one floor, which means that their occupants lived in them for no more than 25 to 30 years. The original settlers must have shortly been joined by other Achaeans, who brought with them a new style of pottery (Mycenaean IIIC:Ib), which was subsequently copied when the settlers of Maa-Palaeokastro left this small outpost and moved to a more urban area. The same kind of pottery is found at Palaepaphos, which is the nearest large urban centre. We suggest that these Achaeans, having established themselves safely at Maa and having surveyed the surrounding area, gradually occupied Palaepaphos, which was an already flourishing Late Cypriot II town. The same pattern may be observed in the eastern part of Cyprus where the Achaeans may have settled for a while in the plain of Sinda, before moving to occupy the large town of Enkomi.

During this troubled period, commercial relations with the peoples of the Aegean ceased and the Myceaean pottery style died out in Cyprus. It was replaced by a new local style which, in its initial stages, was greatly influenced by carved ivory and bronze plaques. The Oriental influence of carving is evidenced by the use of thick lines for the outlines of figured motifs, and thin lines for anatomical details. The most favoured compositions were bulls and goats eating from bushes, a theme which was also popular in ivory carving. This style soon degenerated, however, and became very careless, hence the name "Rude Style" which was given to it. However, we prefer to call it "Pastoral", considering that "Rude" does not do justice to some very delicately-rendered compositions.

The upheavals in the Eastern Mediterranean caused by the Sea Peoples are reflected in an illuminating series of "letters" between the king of Ugarit Hammourapi and the king of Alashiya. They exchange information about the movement of enemy ships near their shores and give advice to one another on how to face the situation.

The nature of the settlement of the first Achaeans in Cyprus is not very clear. Obviously, their primary aim was to establish themselves in the island's main urban areas. Although this may not have been achieved without resentment from the local population, it seems that it was a rather peaceful process. At any rate, the signs of their presence are virtually everywhere. For example, at Enkomi, too, traces of a "cyclopean" wall have been found. The wall circles almost all of the town. It had towers at regular intervals along its south, west, and north sides. Now that the limits of the city wall are known, it is possible to calculate the size of the city, which was c.400m by 300m.

A new kind of town planning was introduced at Enkomi by the invaders. There is a very regular grid of streets which cross the town from one end to the other. The streets connect opposite gates and intersect at right angles. At about the centre of the town there is an open square paved with stone slabs.

For the first time monumental buildings other than fortresses appeared on Cyprus. At Enkomi, a large building, perhaps a palace, was discovered. It is built of large well-dressed blocks of hard limestone, called "ashlars", which are 3 m. in length and 1.40 m. in height. Although this method of construction coincides with the arrival of the Achaean colonists on Cyprus, it cannot possibly have been introduced by them from the Greek Mainland, since there was no monumental architecture of this style in Greece at that time. Most likely it originated in Anatolia or Ugarit —a likely hypothesis, since it is known that refugees from Ugarit fled to Cyprus after the destruction of their city. Indeed, Ugaritan builders may have been used for the construction of these new buildings.

The "palace" of Enkomi, known in archaeological literature as "Building 18", is a rectangular structure opening to streets on all four sides. Its main facade is 40 m. long, with spacious doors and windows. There are a number of rooms round a central courtyard.

The same methods of construction were used for the building of sanctuaries. At Enkomi there are three major sanctuaries dating to the Late Cypriot III period. The largest is the sanctuary of the "Horned God". It consists of a large rectangular hall whose roof was supported on two rectangular stone pillars. There was an altar and a table of offerings in the hall. Around the altars were large numbers of bowls used for pouring libations, as well as the skulls of oxen and other horned animals, which were sacrificed to the god. Their skulls were then placed against the walls of the sanctuary, though some of the skulls may have been used as masks worn by the priests and worshippers during ritual performances. From the hall one could proceed to two inner cult rooms. In one of these rooms a most important discovery was made, namely the bronze statue of a Horned God. This work, some 55 cm. tall, is the largest statue yet found from this period. Its muscular torso and youthful features express beauty and divine serenity — the forerunner of Greek Archaic sculpture.

The second major sanctuary at Enkomi is of a quite different sort. It consists of a propylaeum and a cella (a forecourt and a main court). There was a rectangular free-standing pillar in the central part of the main court, but only the stone base and the capital survive. A well was adjacent to the pillar. The pillars had a religious significance in Aegean sacred architecture which suggests that this sanctuary may have been influenced by the architectural ideas of the Achaean colonists. The stone capital with its stepped profile and cavity is a type known from other sanctuaries of the same period at Myrtou-Pigadhes, Kition and Palaepaphos.

The third sanctuary, which was built c.1150 B.C., was not constructed with ashlar blocks, but with rubble. It consists of a rectangular cella, in which there was a hearth altar and two freestanding blocks of stone. One was pierced for tethering sacrificial animals, which were slaughtered on the concave top of the other block. On the floor excavators found the skulls of numerous oxen and other horned animals. There is a small cella in the north-eastern corner of the courtyard. Here, another bronze statue of the cult god was found. This is known as the sanctuary of the "Ingot God", since the god is represented standing on a base shaped like a copper ingot. There were benches against the walls of the courtyard, where offerings were deposited.

Sanctuaries have also been discovered at Kition. The Near Eastern character of these is obvious. Their general plan recalls that of the sanctuaries of Lachish, Tel Qasile and Tel Farah in Palestine. The Kition sanctuaries are clustered in the northern part of the town, near the gate in the north-east corner of the city wall. It might seem strange to have so many sanctuaries near the wall, but this happens to be the arrangement in other places in the Near East as well as in the Aegean, the idea being to situate the sanctuaries so that during annual ceremonies divinities could "properly" enter the city they were supposed to protect through the city gate.

By the Late Cypriot II period, two sanctuaries and a sacred garden had been built in the same area. One of them (Temple 3) was demolished during the Late Cypriot III period and its foundations were covered by the floor of an open-air sacred courtyard (*temenos*), while the other (Temple 2) was slightly remodelled and its walls were constructed of ashlar blocks. A large temple (Temple 1) was then constructed; it measures 33.60 m. by 22 m. and consists of a large rectangular courtyard with a passage along its south side. Along the west side was a long narrow corridor which must have been roofed. It is connected with the courtyard through three openings.

The narrow corridor was the holy of holies or sanctum sanctorum, a place where the image of the divinity and the sacred vessels were kept. Nothing is known about the nature of this divinity, because the same temple was reused during the Phoenician period, and the earliest floors were removed down to the bedrock, so almost nothing of the Late Cypriot III period was found. In the courtyard, however, there were pits for a sacred garden and a well for irrigation. A rectangular pool where sacred fishes may have been kept was similar to "sacred temple lakes" for deities found in some Egyptian temples of the same period.

Temple 1 is one of the largest Late Bronze Age sanctuaries found in the Mediterranean. Its south facade was built of large ashlar blocks with drafted edges, which rest on long narrow blocks with a central boss. There are indications that there was at least one more course of blocks above them. These blocks are quite large; they are 1.50 m. high and some of them measure 3.50 m. in length. Graffiti of ships were traced on this facade, which was quite appropriate for a harbour town whose economy was based on export trade. There were two lateral entrances to the temple courtyard. The one on the east side was a kind of propylaeum with two holes in the paved floor which supported poles for banners, as was the fashion in Egyptian temples. The entrance on the south side had a staircase and a ramp.

There is an open courtyard (*temenos A*) along the north side of Temple 1 in which there was a low sacrificial altar with a cemented top, and a table of offerings, next to which stone "horns of consecration" were found, a religious symbol which must have been introduced by the Achaeans. A second open courtyard, *temenos B*, existed along the east facade of Temple 1, with a portico along its south side, and a roof supported by two pillars whose stone bases and capitals were found on the floor. This temenos, like temenos A, had a pair of horns which were reused as building material in a later wall.

Temples 1 and 2, with the two sacred courtyards, formed a single architectural unit entered through a spacious propylaeum from the east. The "door" of this propylaeum is impressive, as it is 4.20 m. wide. The east facade of the architectural unit, built of ashlar blocks, measures 23.50 m. in length. A street runs along the east and the south, thus giving access to the principal gates of the building.

East of this architectural unit are two other temples, designated 4 and 5. They are separated from the first architectural unit by an open space and from one another by a street which leads to the adjacent city gate. Temple 4 has a rectangular courtyard, with an altar and a table of offerings in the middle. Along its east side is a holy of holies which is divided into two compartments. In one of them a hoard of ivory objects was found. They include an inscribed pipe used for smoking opium. In Temple 5 there was a cylindrical vase which may have been used for burning opium and inhaling the smoke. This vase is similar to one found in the sanctuary of the "opium goddess" at Gazi in Crete. It is known that opium was exported from Cyprus to Egypt during the Late Bronze Age, perhaps for medical use in temples.

On the floor of the other compartment were bowls used for pouring libations. Temple 4 has two entrances: one on the east and the other on the west. The east portal leads to an open paved area, the surface of which is heavily burnt. This area may have contained a sacrificial altar which was destroyed when a Hellenistic water reservoir was built. Temple 4 was constructed with small ashlar blocks. Only the foundations of the other walls, which were built of stone anchors, survive. In the north-west corner of the courtyard, below the floor, a "foundation deposit" was discovered. It consists of two bronze agricultural tools and one large bronze peg, recalling the inscribed clay pegs found in the foundations of Babylonian temples. The peg, found in the Kition excavation, was meant to symbolise the structural solidity of the temple.

Very little is known about the divinity who was worshipped in Temple 4 during the Late Cypriot III period. In the 11th century B.C., however, a goddess of fertility was worshipped, if one is to judge from a terracotta figure found on the floor of the courtyard, which represents a female goddess with uplifted arms.

Temple 5 is smaller and "ruder" than temple 4. It was constructed of rubble with a small holy of holies on its west side. Against the parapet wall is a rectangular table for offerings. A stone anchor, found leaning against the south side of this table, was obviously dedicated by a sailor in honour of the Baal (god) of sailors, before he departed on a long voyage.

There were two porticos along the north and south walls of the courtyard, the roofs of which were supported by wooden pillars. Their stone bases survive on the floor. Traces of hearth altars were found along the middle of the floor. Smoke from these altars exited the courtyard through an opening between the porticos. There was a lateral entrance near the north-east corner, with a table for offerings next to it. On the floor of the temple several skulls of oxen and other horned animals were found, as was an upright stone anchor. The divinity who was worshipped in this temple must have been a male god to judge from the *bucrania* (skulls of oxen) and the anchors, which are usually dedicated to a Baal.

The sacred architecture of Kition is directly related to and connected with an "industrial" quarter adjacent to it. In fact one could walk from Temple 1 to a workshop used for copper smelting, which was situated between the temple and the city wall. This workshop is connected to three others. The workshops were open to the sky, so fumes resulting from smelting could be blown away by the prevalent southern winds. The copper itself was kept under canopies. Several small furnaces and fragments of crucibles, bellows and other smelting implements were found on the floors, mixed with charcoal, ashes and copper slag. There is evidence that there was some metallurgical activity in this area during the Late Cypriot II period, but these earlier workshops have not been located yet.

The melding of the sacred and the industrial is also found at Temple 1, where a series of workshops have been uncovered behind the holy of holies. They were either connected with the temple as workshops for weaving, grinding corn, etc., or were used for smelting. A number of these workshops contain pits for storing bone ash, which was used as a fluxing material during the smelting process.

Another major religious structure of the Late Cypriot III period is the temple of Aphrodite at Palaepaphos. The date of its construction, c. 1200 B.C., has been established by recent excavations, which scotched the notion that it was a Roman edifice. Only very few architectural remains are preserved, since the temple was in continuous use down to the Roman period. Its walls were built with enormous ashlar blocks, like those used in Temple 1 at Kition. There is evidence that there were rectangular stone pillars in what may have been a courtyard. There is also evidence that there was some metallurgical activity in the area of the temple. The comparison with the Kition temples is strengthened even further by the presence of stone "horns of consecration".

Fortunately for archaeologists, the plan of the temple of

Aphrodite is depicted on Roman coins struck in Cyprus. The temple has a tripartite holy of holies with a courtyard in front of it — an arrangement not unlike that of Temple 1 at Kition. In the central cella, a conical object appears which could be identified with the large conical grey stone found many years ago in the temple area. This may have been a stone sacred to Aphrodite that survived from prehistoric times.

Finally, there is a small sanctuary near Athienou (Golgoi), a town half-way between Kition and Nicosia. The sanctuary was built in the 14th century B.C. and was in continuous use until the Late Cypriot III period. On its floor hundreds of miniature vessels were found, as well as numerous nodules of copper, and bronze objects. There is no doubt that here, too, was a cult connected with metallurgy. This is not surprising, considering that Golgoi was on the route which connected Kition to the mining areas of north-west Cyprus.

The basis of prehistoric religion in Cyprus has always been a fertility divinity. In the Chalcolithic period this divinity was represented by a nude female figure; in the Early and Middle Bronze Ages by a woman holding an infant. The conservative Cypriots retained these religious figures well into the Late Bronze Age. There are numerous terracottas from this period representing a nude female figure holding an infant or pressing her breasts. There are also bull figures in clay or bronze, sometimes accompanied by human figures who lead them to be sacrificed. The male divinity is represented by a human figure only during the Late Cypriot III period, with the "Horned God" or the "Ingot God", both of which were found in sanctuaries at Enkomi.

The "Horned God" is youthful, and is represented in an attitude which recalls Near Eastern prototypes. He is standing, with one arm bent against his chest and the other extended in front of him with the palm of the hand open and turned downwards. He wears a horned cap of animal's skin and a kilt. This deity, which succeeded the old Cypriot god of fertility whose symbol was the bull, has been identified with Apollo Alasiotas (the god of Alashiya), after a reference to him in a 4th century B.C. inscription found at Tamassos. He was also known as Apollo Keraeatas (with horns), a deity that was worshipped in Arcadia as a god of cattle and patron of shepherds. References to Apollo Keraeatas appear in a Hellenistic inscription from Pyla, near Kition. The fact that several skulls of horned animals were found on the floor of his temple at Enkomi may lend support to the identification of Keraeatas, since it is known that some of the Achaean colonists came from Arcadia.

The "Ingot God" is fully armed. He carries a shield and a spear, wears a horned helmet, greaves and a short tunic. The fact that he stands on a base in the form of an ox-hide ingot not only earned him his name, but also his identification with the god who protected the copper mines of Cyprus. The Ashmolean Museum at Oxford some years ago acquired a small bronze statuette of Cypriot origin, dating to the 12th century B.C. and representing a nude female goddess standing on a base in the form of an ox-hide ingot. She has been identified with the Goddess who symbolised the fertility of the mines. Thus we have two divinities in Cyprus during the 12th century B.C., a male and a female, both associated with metallurgy. Since the island's economy was based on the export of copper, it is not surprising that the Cypriots invented divinities to protect this essential material.

Votive ingots, some of them inscribed, have been found at Enkomi. This further illuminates the association of metallurgy with religion at Kition, Palaepaphos, Myrtou and Athienou. Nor is this phenomenon confined only to Cyprus; it is also encountered in the Near East and can even be traced to Greek mythology, where Hephaestos, the smith-god, is the consort of Aphrodite. The Ingot God of Enkomi and the Ingot Goddess in the Ashmolean Museum may in fact be their predecessors.

Although the Achaean colonists were firmly established by the 12th century B.C. in the urban centres of Cyprus, their influence on the island's religion was not spectacular. Apart from the introduction of the "Horns of Consecration" and perhaps the pillar cult, the main elements of Cypriot religion during the Late Cypriot III period are based on old Cypriot, rather than on Achaean traditions. This phenomenon may be explained by the reluctance of Cypriots to embrace new theologies and also by the slow process of colonisation. In fact, it appears that the Achaeans adopted a number of elements from Cypriot religion and religious architecture.

From objects discovered in the various Late Cypriot III sanctuaries one may draw some tentative conclusions as to the character of the rituals performed in these sanctuaries. In most of the sanctuaries, bowls have been found round altars, which indicate that libations were offered. Carbonised bones and sacrificial altars are evidence of animal sacrifices. Usually bulls were killed, but there were also deer, as the bones of these animals have been found at Enkomi and Kition. Incense-burners have been found in most sanctuaries as well as tables for bloodless gifts like fruit.

The custom of wearing *bucrania* during ritual performances survived down to the Archaic period, as can be seen from terracotta and stone representations from Kourion and elsewhere.

Votive clay masks dated to c.1050 B.C. and found in deposits near Temple 5 suggest that such anthropomorphic masks were worn during ritual performances at Kition. Similar masks have been found at other sacred sites in the Near East — e.g. Tell Qasile and Hazor in Palestine. Others have been found in the sanctuary of the Ingot God. As for the Goddess of fertility, her Cretan origin is undeniable. The deity must have been introduced by Cretan immigrants who settled as refugees on the east and south-east coasts of Cyprus, having fled from Crete after the "Dorian invasion" from the Balkans in c. 1100 B.C.

If anything, the contribution of the Achaean settlers in the secular area is more conspicuous than in the religious one.

First of all, they introduced to the island new and advanced metallurgical techniques.

The two bronze statues found at Enkomi, described previously, are characteristic of the new Achaean art. Of particular interest are the Greek facial characteristics of the Horned God, which became a staple of Archaic Greek art some six centuries later. Bronze figurines of human figures, bulls and other quadrupeds are abundant from this period.

Bronze vases must have been numerous during the Achaean period, but few have survived. There are, however, some spectacular examples, in particular the cast handles and rims of three large amphorae, which are decorated with *genii* holding ewers, and which depict octopuses, bulls and so forth — all of them rendered in a very realistic manner.

Equally important is the realistic style of the relief or cut-out decoration of four-sided stands supported on wheels. These remarkable objects have relief decoration (usually animals), on the flat ring at the top of the stands, and four rectangular panels on the sides which are decorated in the cut-out technique with various compositions —chariot groups, human figures in various compositions (one playing a lyre, another carrying an ox-hide ingot on his shoulders). A stand recently acquired by the Cyprus Museum, probably from the Kourion area, has four identically-decorated panels, each with three registers, decorated in the cut-out technique with fighting animals — lions, bulls and griffins — which correspond almost exactly to the biblical description of the bronze stands made for King Solomon (1 *Kings* 7, 27-30), in the 10th century B.C. Wheeled stands are mentioned by Homer in the *Iliad* as having been made by Hephaestos for the banquets of the gods. But the style of the stands found in Cyprus shows them to be of undeniably Cypriot origin. They were imitated in later periods both by the Cretans and by the Etruscans.

A similar cut-out technique was used in ivory carvings, which must have flourished in Cyprus during the 12th century

B.C., as there is evidence of ivory workshops at Palaepaphos and Kition. Several fine specimens of this work have been found in Cyprus. A plaque showing the Egyptian god Bes, which was found in the holy of holies in Kition Temple 4 is designed so it can be seen from both sides, and the *tenons* (tabs) on either end of the plaque suggest that it was originally conceived as a decorative part of a piece of furniture. Also from Temple 4 is another ivory plaque cut out in the form of a springing lion. The technique and style recall Aegean pro-totypes. Of more certain Aegean inspiration are the two bulls sitting under an olive tree, as shown in relief on one of the short sides of an ivory draught box from Enkomi. The long sides are decorated in relief with scenes of animal-hunting from a chariot in Near Eastern style. There are two ivory mirror handles from Enkomi and Palaepaphos respectively. Their broad flat upper portions are decorated in relief with scenes which include a "hero" fighting a lion and a griffin and a bull attacked by a lion. A small plaque from Kition shows a seated woman holding a mirror.

Glyptics (carvings on hard stones) continue the fine tradi-tion of the Late Cypriot II period, except that there is more emphasis on the conoid stamp seals, on which pictorial motifs appear such as bulls, stags and human figures. These figures often exhibit a strong Aegean influence.

In jewellery a new technique, called *cloisonné*, was intro-duced during this period and appears on several finger rings from Palaepaphos. In *cloisonné*, the circular bezel was divided by thin sheets of gold into various curvilinear patterns, which were filled with white enamel. The surface then was smoothed so that both the enamel and the thin gold section were visible. The same technique was used to decorate a gold sceptre found in a royal tomb at Kourion-Kaloriziki (11th century B.C.). The sceptre consists of a globe topped by two falcons, and is decorated with blue and white enamel. The tubular shaft con-sists of a thin sheet of gold.

The diverse ceramic styles used during the Late Cypriot II period evolve into a rather austere style which imitates Mycenaean pottery made in the 12th century B.C. Its repertory is very limited, the prevalent form being the deep bowl with opposed horizontal loop handles known as a *skyphos*. The space between the handles is usually decorated with antithetic spirals or other abstract motifs, and human and animal forms are included on larger vases, though these are nothing like the exuberant compositions wrought by Mycenaean artists of the 14th and 13th centuries.

Some Cypriot vase-painters, however, produced a rather heavily ornate style, which appears mainly on large craters. The surface of these vases is divided into numerous rectangular panels and horizontal zones which are filled with linear geometric motifs but occasionally also with fishes, birds and quadrupeds. This style has been characteristically called "pleonastic".

Such art-making did not, of course, take place in a vacuum. During the second half of the 12th century, a catastrophe struck both Kition and Enkomi — and was followed by the intro-duction of a new style of pottery which is called the "Granary style", after the pottery style in use when the granary of the Mycenaean acropolis was destroyed. Scholars have suggested that these catastrophes may have resulted from continued struggle between the indigenous population and Achaean settlers, who were joined by larger and larger numbers of their kinspeople.

Cretans joined this new influx of settlers, and brought with them several characteristic art styles; for instance, the sub-Mi-noan style in vase-painting which included the goddess with uplifted arms referred to earlier. This goddess is quite dist-inctive. It has a high flat headdress (*polos*), swollen eyes, a pointed nose, large ears, and wears necklaces and bracelets. There are usually painted spots on the goddess' cheeks. This deity spread all over Cyprus.

The second wave of Achaean colonists introduced to Cyprus a new ceramic style known as Proto-White Painted or Proto-Bichrome. Its forms and decorative patterns are predominantly Aegean (inspired from sub-Minoan and sub-Mycenaean pottery), but there are also Near Eastern and local Cypriot elements.

After the destruction of the Syrian cities by the Sea Peoples and the settlement of the latter in Palestine, several Syro-Palestinian peoples must have come to Cyprus as refugees, introducing their own ceramic styles. The Syro-Palestinian "Canaanite" jar is imitated in the Proto-White Painted pottery as well as the bottles with long cylindrical bodies. The same mix of influences seen in the shapes of vases is found in their decoration. Orange or dark brown matt paint is applied on a light surface. Sometimes two colours are used — black and purple, for Proto-Bichrome ware. A characteristic example is a deep conical bowl (*kalathos*) from Palaepaphos. The form itself is Aegean. But its decoration — geometric and pictorial motifs like "union jacks", swastikas, rosettes, birds, a lyre-player and a goat with long back-curved horns — reflects both Near Eastern and Aegean artistic influences.

At the cemetery at Alaas, a site in the Karpass peninsula north-east of Salamis, a number of tombs, dating to the first half of the 11th century B.C., have been excavated. These structures, the first tombs of a Mycenaean type found on Cyprus, contain a large quantity of vases of Proto-White Painted and Proto-Bichrome, and also a fair number of imported Syrian flasks. Each tomb has a small rock-cut chamber and a long narrow *dromos*, which is filled with soil and rubble, as is the entrance. Following the Mycenaean custom, there is only one burial space in each tomb. Burial gifts include numerous pieces of pottery and gold jewellery, though not in large quantities. There were also bronze fibulae, and bronze and iron knives and weapons. The D-shaped fibula was introduced from the Aegean.

Iron appeared rather rarely, for knives and other weapons, as early as the 12th century B.C., but did not come into widespread use until the middle of the 11th century B.C.

40
Jug of Bichrome Wheelmade ware. This jug belongs to a class which was previously considered to have been imported from the Syro-Palestinian coast, but recent research has assigned it to Cyprus. It belongs to a style, however, which is well outside the Cypriot ceramic tradition, and may have been produced by foreign craftsmen working in Cyprus, who also introduced to the island the potter's wheel. Its neck is decorated with a human figure armed with a sword and a dagger. The usual motifs of the decoration of such vases are birds and fishes within rectangular panels. Human figures and quadrupeds are very rare.

Early part of the Late Bronze Age. From a tomb at Dromolaxia-'Trypes' (Tomb 1, no.58). Larnaca District Museum. Height: 24 cm.

41

Composite juglet of Base-Ring I ware. It consists of two juglets, the bodies of which are joined. They have a common handle that runs from between their mouths to the point where their bodies join. Such juglets, known as *bilbils*, abundant during the Late Bronze Age, are considered to have the shape of a poppy capsule, and are thought to have contained opium. They are often found outside Cyprus, particularly in Egyptian tombs. The material of these vases is thin and hard and has a metallic texture which no doubt imitates metallic prototypes.

Early part of the Late Bronze Age. Uncertain provenance. Cyprus Museum, Nicosia, no.A1236. Height: 10 cm.

42

A handmade terracotta representing a horse and a rider. The horse is hollow and the human figure is seated sideways on a saddle. Both the rider and the saddle were moulded separately and were added before firing to the horse's body. Black and brown paint is used for rendering details, mainly the facial characteristics of the rider. The sex of the rider is not indicated. The usual animal-shaped terracottas in this style are bulls; horses are very rare and are even more rare with riders. A similar terracotta figure in Mycenaean style was found in a tomb in Attica; it represents a 'goddess' with uplifted arms.

Late Bronze Age (c. 13th century B.C.). Provenance uncertain. Cyprus Museum, Nicosia, no.1979/XII-8/2. Height (with rider): 15.8 cm.

43

Terracotta figurine of a standing nude woman holding an infant in her left arm. She has a bird's face, with a large nose, large ears pierced twice, through which large ear-rings hang. Her eyes are rendered with pellets of clay. Grooves circle the neck and the pubic area. Such terracotta figurines are very frequently found in tombs of the 14th and 13th century B.C. They accompany the dead to the second life, perhaps as a substitute for a real spouse. This type of figure originated in Syria and may be connected with Astarte, the divinity of fertility.

Cyprus Museum, Nicosia, no.1934/IV-27/3.
Height: 21 cm.

44

Aerial view of the excavated remains of Enkomi. The remains, situated near Cyprus' east coast, so far constitute the most important archaeological site of the Cypriot Late Bronze Age. The town had an inner harbour which was connected with the sea through a navigable chanel. Enkomi started as a small community of farmers in the 17th century B.C., but from the 14th century B.C. acquired considerable importance as a result of the development of trade relations with Egypt and the Syro-Palestinian coast. Towards the very end of the 13th century, it was occupied by the Achaean colonists who are responsible for a new town with streets crossing at right angles, a 'cyclopean' wall, and the first public buildings constructed of large hewn blocks of stone (*ashlars*). The city was destroyed by an earthquake or another physical phenomenon in c.1075 B.C., when its inhabitants started to abandon it; they moved to the area near the coast, on a natural harbour, where they built Salamis. Enkomi was first excavated by a British mission at the end of the 19th century. In the 1930s a French mission started excavations and was later joined by the Cyprus Department of Antiquities.

45

Aerial view of the excavated remains of the northernmost part of Kition. The ancient town of Kition lies underneath the houses of the modern town of Larnaca, near the south-east coast. It started as a small settlement during the later part of the Early Bronze Age and became a town with an important harbour only at the beginning of the 13th century B.C., when the coastal towns along the east and south coasts became trading centres. As was the case with Enkomi, copper was exported from its inner harbour to the Aegean and the Near East. At the northernmost part of the town, excavated by the Department of Antiquities since 1962, part of the 'cyclopean' wall of the town was uncovered as well as a complex of workshops and sanctuaries dating from c.1200 B.C. There is a connection between metallurgy and religion, as is also illustrated by the divinities who were worshipped in Cyprus during the later part of the Late Bronze Age (see nos.71,72). This part of Kition was abandoned c.1000 B.C., but was later reoccupied by the Phoenicians, who rebuilt the largest of the Late Bronze Age temples and dedicated it to Astarte.

46

Mycenaean IIIA amphoroid crater, from
Enkomi, decorated on the largest part
of the body with pictorial compositions.
The two main sides of the body between
the handles are occupied by two large
octopuses. The most interesting composition,
however, is placed below one of the handles:
it consists of a chariot group and other figures
in the background; of these, one long-robed
human figure stands in front of the horses,
holding what look like scales. This scene has
been identified with the well-known scene in
the *Iliad*, where Zeus holds the 'scales of
destiny' in front of the warriors before they
depart for battle. If this interpretation is
correct, it is one of the earliest mythological
representations in Aegean vase-painting.
There is a second human figure holding an
unidentifiable object in the foreground, a bull
figure, and floral ornaments. Such
pictorially-decorated vases have been found in
large numbers in the rich tombs of Enkomi
and other Late Bronze Age sites of the 14th
and 13th centuries B.C.

Cyprus Museum, Nicosia, Enkomi Tomb 17,
no.1 (Swedish excavations). Height: 37.5 cm.;
mouth diameter: 26 cm.

47

Mycenaean IIIA open crater from Enkomi, decorated on both sides with a chariot group and a large bird flying behind the chariot. The compositions on this vase, like those on no.46, have been associated with a mythological scene. In Near Eastern mythology a large bird called Anzu or Enzu is said to be chased by heroes over the mountains (shown here by stylised rocks). On this vase the bird is chasing the heroes. On another Mycenaean vase found at Ugarit, the final episode in the story of the Anzu bird is depicted: the bird is finally caught and chained. It is probable that Near Eastern myths circulated in areas like Cyprus, with which the Mycenaeans were in close contact.

Cyprus Museum, Nicosia, Enkomi Tomb 7, no.4784 (French excavations). Height:33 cm; mouth diameter: 34.1 cm.

48
Mycenaean IIIA amphoroid crater from
Enkomi, decorated on the shoulder on both
sides between the handles with bulls and
human figures. On the one side the bulls are
peacefully walking or standing, receiving the
caresses of human figures. On the other side
they are leaping over a rocky landscape. In
this respect they recall the bull scenes on the
famous Vaphio cups from the Peloponnese,
on which two contrasting scenes with bulls are
depicted. Bull figures were very fashionable in
fresco-painting on the Mycenaean mainland
and in Crete, where the vase-painter
ultimately received his inspiration.

Cyprus Museum, Nicosia, Enkomi Tomb 10,
no.200 (Cyprus Department of Antiquities
excavations).
Height: 43.5 cm.; mouth diameter: 31.7 cm.

49
Mycenaean IIIA amphoroid crater, decorated
on both sides with two stylised octopuses
whose symmetrically-arranged tentacles cover
the whole of the vase's body. The octopus was
a much favoured motif of Minoan art. When it
was taken over by the Mycenaeans, it lost its
naturalism and free movement in favour of
stylisation that is a characteristic of Mycenaean
vase-painting.

Cyprus Museum, Nicosia, no.1962/V-31/1.
Height: 34 cm.; mouth diameter: 29 cm.

50

Mycenaean IIIB amphoroid crater from Shemishin (north of Larnaca) decorated on either side between the handles with two lions which stand on either side of a flower motif turning their heads in opposite directions. There are large petalled flowers in the background. This is one of the last amphoroid craters of the Mycenaean IIIB style (13th century B.C.), the shape being confined mainly to the Mycenaean IIIA style (14th century B.C.). The figured motifs by now lose their naturalism and become decorative, hence the exaggeratedly long bodies of the lions, the purpose of which was to fill the whole of the shoulder zone. Compositions with antithetic animals appear in other aspects of Mycenaean art, the best known being that of the stone relief with antithetic lions above the gate on the Acropolis of Mycenae known as the Lion's Gate.

Cyprus Museum, Nicosia, no.A1648.
Height: 41.5 cm.; mouth diameter: 31.5 cm.

51

Mycenaean IIIB bowl, with hemispherical body and wishbone handle. This is a rare shape in the repertory of Mycenaean pottery and most probably imitates a Cypriot form, namely the very common White Slip ware 'milk-bowls'. This, however, raises the problem of the origin of the Mycenaean pottery found in Cyprus. Some scholars believe that there were Mycenaean potters established in the large harbour-towns of Cyprus who were producing Mycenaean pottery for the local clientele and the Near Eastern market whose repertory was occasionally influenced by local pottery.

Cyprus Museum, Nicosia, no.1955/IV-14/2.
Height: 9.5 cm.; diameter: 16 cm.

52

The end of the 13th century B.C. coincides with a troubled period in the Aegean and the Eastern Mediterranean, which caused the discontinuation of Mycenaean pottery reaching Cyprus. It is at this time that local pottery produced a style in imitation of the true Mycenaean pictorial style, which is known as 'Rude Style' or 'Pastoral Style'. The style appears mainly on open craters and its favoured motifs are bulls and goats. This crater is one of the earliest yet found. It shows how much the art of engraving, mainly on

ivory, influenced this style of vase-painting; thin and thick lines are used for rendering anatomical details, particularly on the face and the legs. The crater is decorated on one side with a bull and a goat, on the other side with a bull eating the leaves of a bush. Gradually this style degenerates and becomes very careless.

Cyprus Museum, Nicosia, Enkomi Tomb 19, no.66 (Swedish excavations). Height: 28.7 cm.; mouth diameter: 27.7 cm.

53

Fragment of a clay tablet from Enkomi; the lower part is missing. The tablet is baked and is inscribed with three horizontal rows of signs in the so-called Cypro-Minoan script. The signs were engraved on three horizontal guide-lines before firing. This is the earliest clay tablet so far known from Cyprus. Its script is related to the Linear A script of Crete. The text of the inscription has not yet been deciphered, as it represents an unknown language.

C.1500 B.C. Cyprus Museum, Nicosia, no.1885 (1955 excavations by the Cyprus Department of Antiquities).
Height: 5.5 cm.; width: 7.5 cm.

54

Inscribed clay cylinder. There are 27 inscribed lines on the cylinder, each line containing six or seven signs. It is the only complete long inscription of the Cypro-Minoan script known so far. It dates from the 13th century B.C. Like the previous inscription, the text has not yet been deciphered.

Cyprus Museum, Nicosia. Enkomi (1953 excavations by the Cyprus Department of Antiquities) no.1619.
Length: 5.2 cm.; diameter: 4 cm.

55

Fragmentary clay tablet from Enkomi, inscribed on both sides. This represents about one quarter of a complete cushion-shaped baked tablet. The style of the script, though linear, has been greatly influenced by the cuneiform script. It represents one column of a text, which may be a poem, judging by the unequal length of the lines as seen on the right side of the inscribed column. Unlike the inscribed tablets of the Aegean, which were unbaked and usually represent palace inventories, the tablets of the Cypro-Minoan script have long texts and were baked, following Near Eastern fashions.

13th century B.C. Enkomi (1953 excavations by the Cyprus Department of Antiquities).
Cyprus Museum, Nicosia, no.1687. Preserved height: 10 cm.; preserved width: 9 cm.

56
Gold-plated finger-ring from a tomb at
Enkomi. Its elliptical bezel is engraved with a
lion striding to the right and looking back in
the opposite direction. The lion is
naturalistically rendered, recalling the style of
some of the Aegean gems engraved on stone.

13th century B.C. Cyprus Museum, Nicosia.
Enkomi (Swedish excavations), Tomb 18, no.62
Maximum diameter: 3.2 cm.

57
A gold pendant in the form of a pomegranate,
found in a 13th century B.C. tomb at Enkomi.
At its top is a loop for suspension. Its entire
surrface is decorated with 12 horizontal
parallel rows of small granulated triangles.

Cyprus Museum, Nicosia, no.1954/III-24/1.
Length: 4.7 cm.; diameter: 3.2 cm.

58
A necklace from Ayios Iakovos (Famagusta
District), consisting of eight date-shaped gold
beads and seven beads in the shape of a
pomegranate. There is also a Babylonian
engraved cylinder seal which was used as a
pendant. The form of the beads is Aegean in
character; their association with an Oriental
pendant underlines the mixed character of
Cypriot art during the Late Bronze Age II
period. The necklace was found in a
sanctuary, unlike others which as a rule are
found in tombs as gifts.

Cyprus Museum, Nicosia. Excavations at Ayios
Iakovos by the Swedish Cyprus mission. Total
length of necklace: 19.8 cm.; length of
pendant (including gold cups): 3.7 cm.

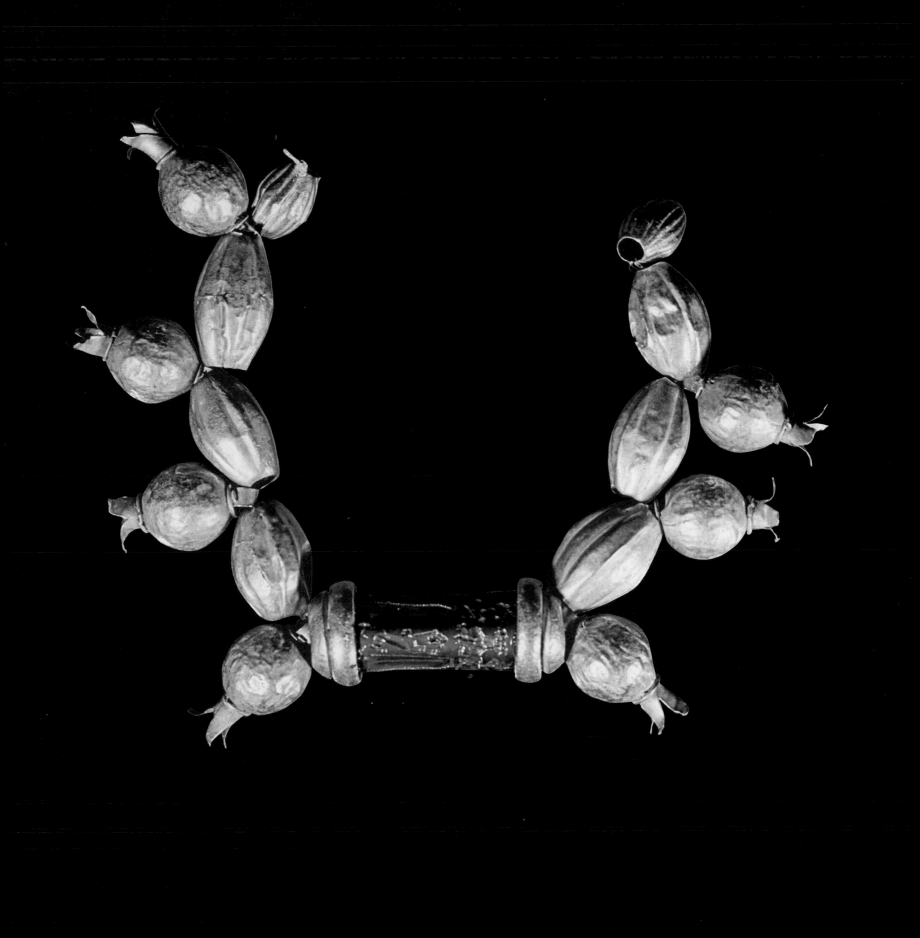

59
Necklace with beads of precious stones and a
gold pendant, from a tomb of the end of the
13th century B.C. and excavated at the Late
Bronze Age site of Hala Sultan Tekké by the
Swedish mission of Göteborg University. The
beads, made of agate, lapis lazuli, carnelian,
etc., are all cupped with gold. The pendant
consists of a circular disc with a hoop at the
top, and is joined with a crescent-shaped
attachment.

Cyprus Museum, Nicosia.
Total length of necklace: 18.5 cm.;
length of pendant: 2.7 cm.
(courtesy of Professor Paul Åström, Göteborg
University).

60
Gold necklace from Enkomi, consisting of 10
large beads in a figure-eight-shaped
shield of Aegean type and separated from one
another by triple cylindrical spacers of gold
wire. The large beads are hollow, and consist
of two embossed sheets of gold.

Found in a 13th century B.C. tomb. Cyprus
Museum, Nicosia. Enkomi (Swedish
excavations), Tomb 18, no.20.
Total length of necklace: 31.7 cm.

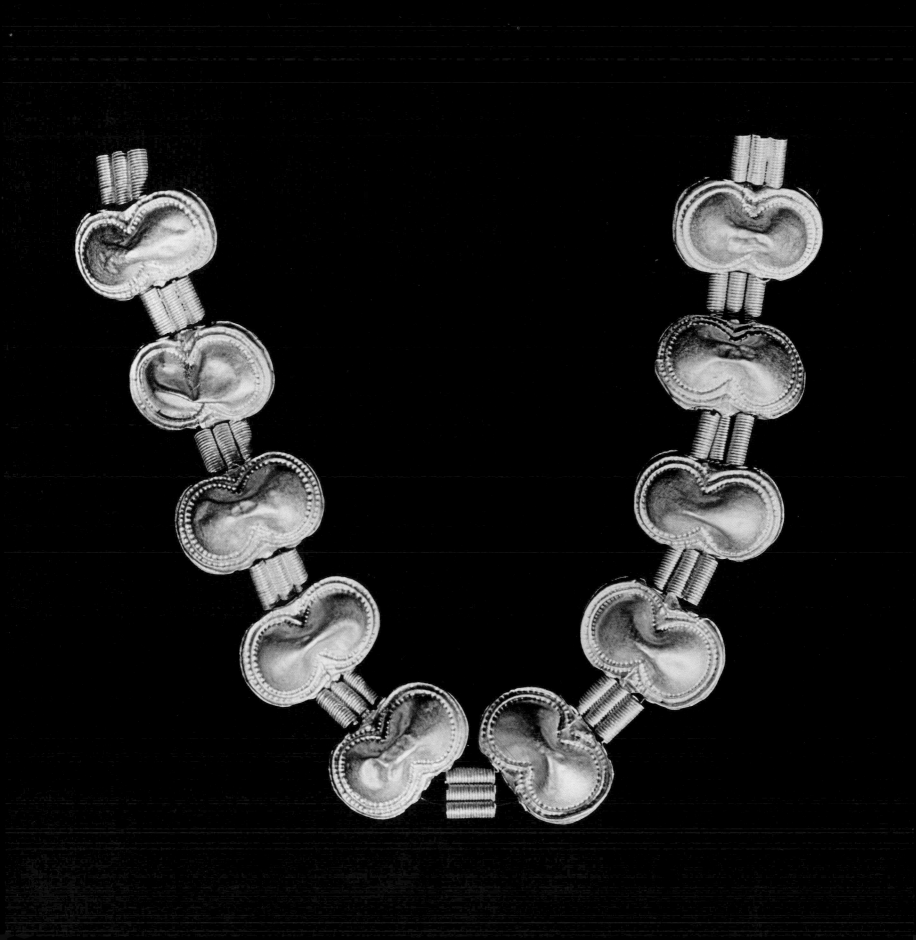

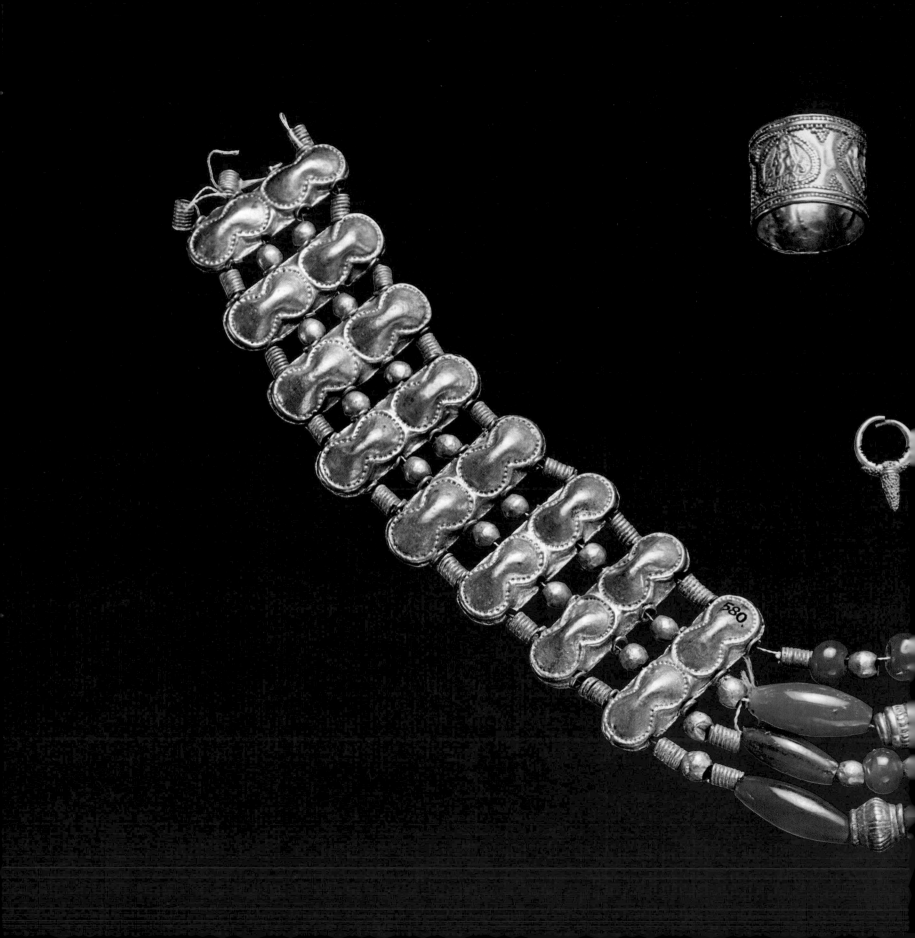

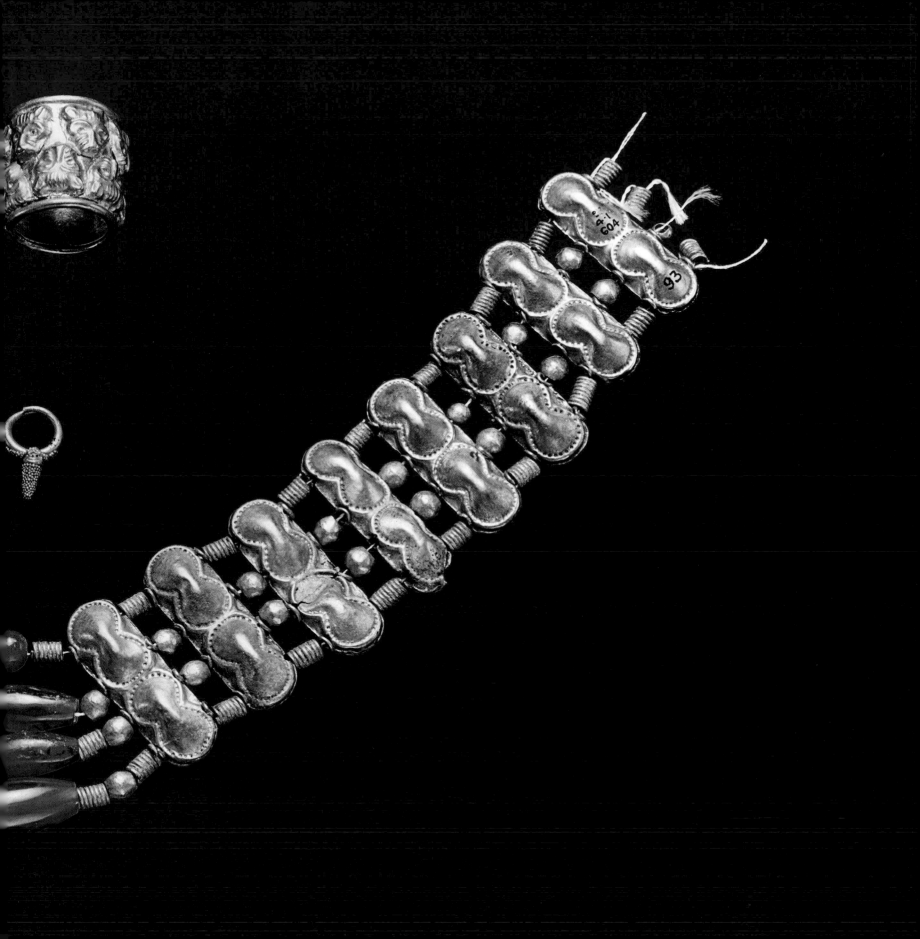

(61-64 on previous pages)

61

Gold ring consisting of a broad band with a gold ring soldered at either end. The band is decorated with two rows of embossed opposed lion's heads, six in each row.

13th century B.C. From Enkomi (British Museum excavations), Tomb 93. British Museum, London, no.583. Diameter: 2 cm.

62

Gold ring consisting of a broad band decorated with four embossed bulls' heads, arranged alternately in opposite directions. The bulls have long curling horns. Along the edges of the ring are granulated small triangles, plain wires and globules.

13th century B.C. From Enkomi (British Museum excavations). British Museum, London, no.582. Diameter: 1.5 cm.

63

Pair of gold ear-rings in the form of a bucranium, the top of which is soldered on a hoop with overlapping ends. The bucranium is covered with granulated decorations.

13th century B.C. British Museum, London, no.543-544. Enkomi Tomb 19 (British Museum excavations). Height: 1.5 cm.

64

Gold necklace from Enkomi. It consists of 16 large beads in the form of a double figure-of-eight shield, perforated four times and separated from one another by smaller gold beads which horizontally are globular or cylindrical. If the restoration of the necklace is correct, then the middle part consists of six large amygdaloid beads of carnelian and other smaller beads, of gold and carnelian. The exuberant character of this necklace and the amount of gold it contains is characteristic of the wealth of the inhabitants of Enkomi gained through trade in copper during the 14th and 13th centuries B.C.

British Museum, London. Enkomi (British Museum excavations), Tomb 93, no.604. Length of large beads: 3.5 cm. Total length: 2.6 cm.

65

Silver bowl found in a 14th century B.C. tomb at Enkomi. It has a hemispherical body, flat base, plain rim, and a 'wishbone' upcurved handle, which is rivetted to the body. The main part of the outside of the bowl is decorated with a horizontal frieze of six heads of oxen. The whole decoration is inlaid in gold and a black substance known as *niello* with a pair of lotus flowers between them. The lower part is decorated with a horizontal frieze of petalled rosettes, each within a semicircle. There is a row of dots round the upper part of the body below the rim; the inside of the bowl is plain. The handle is also decorated in the inlaid technique. This is a rare style of decoration; the nearest parallel to this bowl has been found at Dendra in the Peloponnese.

Cyprus Museum, Nicosia. Enkomi (excavations by the French mission), Tomb 2, no.4207. Height: 6 cm.; diameter: 15.7 cm.

66

Conical rhyton of hard faience, from Kition, covered inside and outside with a thick layer of blue enamel. The handle and the lower part are missing. The outside surface is divided by horizontal parallel ridges into three sections, each of which is decorated. The upper and middle ridges are filled with a frieze of animals and a composition with animals and hunters respectively; the lower one is filled with a vertical row of running spirals. The decoration is in three colours: yellow and black paint, or red inlaid enamel. The upper register contains a frieze of two galloping bulls and a goat; the middle one, two hunters dressed in an Oriental kilt and wearing an Oriental head-dress; one of them wears the 'magic knives' of Egypt on his sandals. The style of the decoration is mixed (Aegean and Near Eastern); the technique is Near Eastern, the form of the vase being Aegean.

From Kition, special series no.1, found outside a tomb. Second half of the 13th century B.C. Cyprus Museum, Nicosia. Preserved height: 26.8 cm.; mouth diameter: 11.9 cm.

67

Silver cup from a tomb at Enkomi, with convex
sides, flat base and horizontal grooves round
the body. The horizontal handle is rivetted on
the body. This cup bears a striking similarity to
the well-known cups from Vaphio in the
Peloponnese, which suggests that it may have
been imported from the Aegean.

Late Bronze Age II period. British Museum,
London (British Museum excavations),
no.1897/4-1/506. Height: 6.9 cm.;
diameter: 10.9 cm.

68

Bronze jug from Enkomi. Ovoid body, long
concave neck, beak-shaped mouth, flat raised
handle from rim to shoulder fixed with rivets,
with a raised splayed foot and a flat base.
Bronze vases are quite rare, either because
they do not survive in good condition or
because they were often melted down as
scrap metal, even in antiquity.

12th century B.C. From a tomb at Enkomi
(British Museum excavations). British Museum,
London, no.1897/4-1/1533. Height: 30.8 cm.

69
Bronze figurine from Ayios Iakovos (Famagusta District), representing a lion seated on its hind legs. Rich mane indicated by grooves; depressions for the eyes and mouth. The animal is rendered very naturalistically.

12th century B.C. Medelhavsmuseet, Stockholm, no.36. Height: 5.5 cm.

70
Bronze statue cast in massive metal, from
Enkomi. The statue represents a youthful god,
standing in a frontal position. The body is
muscular and athletic, with thick legs and bare
feet. The right arm is bent forward with the
palm of the hand turned downward; the right
arm, with a clenched fist, is bent against the
chest. The facial characteristics are very
regular and youthful, recalling some works of
archaic Greek art. The god wears a fleecy
conical helmet with two upcurved horns
springing from the sides and a short kilt
belted round the waist. This is the largest
bronze statue found so far from the Late
Bronze Age of Cyprus. It was discovered in a
sanctuary from the very end of the 13th
century B.C. at Enkomi and may have been the
cult statue of a divinity associated with cattle
and fertility. This god has been identified with
Apollo Keraeatas (horned god) of Arcadia or
Apollo Alasiotas (of Alashiya); it is also
associated with the Near Eastern Baal Reshef.

Cyprus Museum, Nicosia (Cyprus Department
of Antiquities excavations, 1948), no.19.
Height: 54.2 cm.

Bronze statue of a human figure, from
Enkomi. The statue is cast solid and stands in
a frontal position on a base in the form of an
oxhide ingot. The figure is bearded and wears
a conical helmet with horns springing from
the sides. The left arm is extended forward
and holds a small round shield; the right arm
is bent upwards, brandishing a spear. It wears
a close-fitting vest and a kilt; the legs are
protected by greaves. This statue was found in
a 12th century B.C. sanctuary, and was no
doubt the cult statue of a divinity that
protected the copper mines of Cyprus, hence
the ingot base.

Cyprus Museum, Nicosia. Enkomi (1963 French
Mission excavations), no.16.15. Height: 35 cm.

Bronze statuette of a solid cast female figure,
standing on a base in the form of an oxhide
ingot. The figure is nude, with prominent
breasts and a pubic area clearly indicated with
grooves. The arms are missing, but both
hands are placed on either side of the belly
below the breasts, in an attitude which recalls
the figurines of Astarte. It has a flat head,
large ears, grooved facial characteristics and
twisted locks of hair (one is missing), which
fall on the shoulders. It wears a long necklace
reaching its navel. Found in Syria but of
indisputedly Cypriot origin, the 12th century
B.C. statuette has been identified with the
divinity symbolising the fertility of the mines
of Cyprus, and may thus be the companion of
the Ingot God (no.71).

Ashmolean Museum, Oxford, Bomford
Collection. Height: 9.9 cm.

73,74
Aerial photographs of the promontory of Maa-Palaeokastro, on the west coast of Cyprus, north of Paphos. This promontory, measuring c.150 m. in maximum width, was fortified as early as the end of the 13th century B.C. by the earliest Greek colonists who reached Cyprus from the Aegean, and who used it as a military outpost before gradually moving inland to occupy the major urban centre of Palaepaphos. The sides of the promontory are abrupt and provide a natural defence. The Achaeans built a 'cyclopean' wall 4 m. thick both across the neck of the promontory and at the tip, where the land is low, and thus protected the whole plateau where the camp was built. The houses of the settlement were modest; they have only one floor since their occupation did not last for long. Excavations here started in 1954 and were resumed in 1979 and 1980 by the Cyprus Department of Antiquities. (Photo courtesy of the Royal Air Force, Akrotiri, and the Public Information Office, Cyprus.)

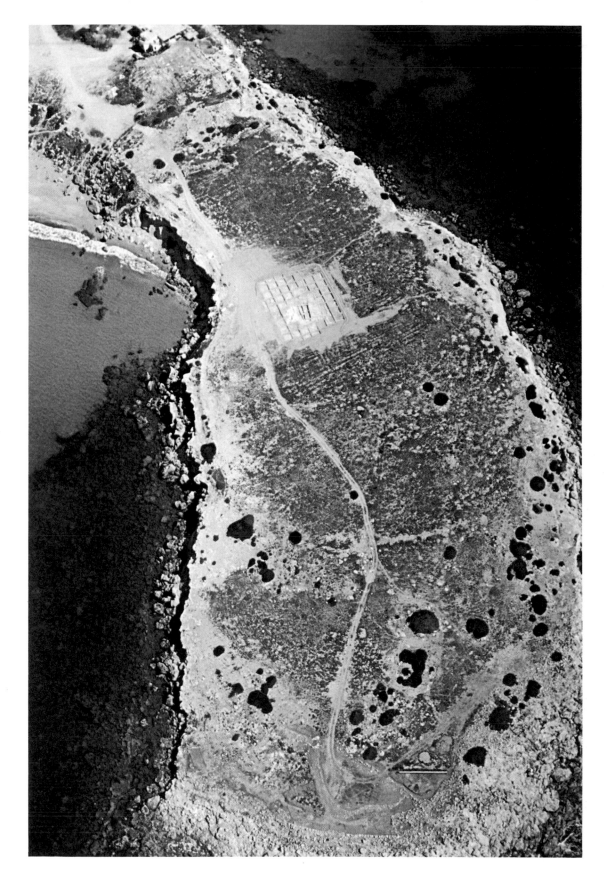

75

Cylindrical ivory pipe found in the 'holy of holies' of Temple 4 at Kition. About one third of the pipe is tubular, with an outlet on the side which is scorched by fire; the rest of the body is solid. At the opposite end there is a string-hole for suspension. The whole surface is engraved with concentric semicircles, zigzag lines and small circles; there is also a long engraved inscription in the Cypro-Minoan script. No doubt this was a pipe for smoking which was used during ritual performances. It is the earliest pipe for smoking — obviously opium — known so far. We know that Cyprus exported opium to Egypt during the Late Bronze Age (see no.41).

C.1200 B.C. Cyprus Museum, Nicosia.
Length: 14 cm.

76

Ivory plaque from the 'holy of holies' of Temple 4 at Kition. It is carved on both sides, in the cut-out (*ajouré*) technique and represents the Egyptian god Bes. It has tenons above and below which suggest that the plaque may have originally been intended to decorate a piece of furniture. There is an engraved inscription in the Cypro-Minoan script along the lower tenon. The god Bes is represented in his usual form, wearing a lion's skin; the lion's tail is missing, and there are snakes in his mouth; he is also wearing a feathered crown. He raises his left arm, brandishing a long feather. This is one of the earliest representations of Bes yet found in Cyprus.

C.1200 B.C. Cyprus Museum, Nicosia.
Height: 22 cm.

Ivory mirror handle from a tomb at
Palaepaphos. It consists of a flat rectangular
section, on which a metallic mirror disc was
fixed, and a cylindrical shaft. The flat
rectangular section is engraved on both sides
with a composition in relief representing a
warrior, wearing a short kilt and armed with a
dagger with which he is stabbing a rampant
lion. The cylindrical shaft is decorated in relief
with vertical rows of stylised foliage. Similar
mirror handles are known from Enkomi and
Kition.

End of the 13th century B.C. Cyprus Museum,
Nicosia. Palaepaphos, site Evreti, Tomb 8,
nos.7.26.34 (British Museum excavations).
Height: 21.5 cm.

78

Ivory draught-box found in a tomb at Enkomi. All four sides of the box are decorated in relief with pictorial compositions. The lid has linear carvings and was used as a gaming board. The box is supported on four short legs. The two long sides are decorated with a scene of hunting from a chariot; there is a hunter in the chariot and a charioteer. The hunter shoots arrows towards a herd of goats and bulls, which gallop in front of the horses. Behind the chariot, a human figure on foot holds an axe. He wears a feathered helmet, characteristic of the Philistines. A dog participates in the hunting, and is shown in

the foreground running near the horses. The two short sides are decorated with two 'couchant' bulls under an olive tree and two goats on either side of a tree respectively. The bulls and the olive tree are rendered in a naturalistic, Aegean style. The rest of the decoration is of a Near Eastern character. This is one of the best specimens of Cypriot ivory carving of the 12th century B.C.

British Museum, London, Turner Bequest, 1897.4-1.996. Enkomi (1896 British Museum excavations), Tomb 58.
Length: 29 cm.; width: 7.5 cm.; height: 8.5 cm.

79

A clay crucible from Enkomi. Coarse clay, thick walls, cylindrical body, flat base, with a layer of copper inside the crucible. Such vessels were used for melting metal. Extensive installations for the smelting of copper have been found at Enkomi and Kition. The copper must have been carried to the main harbour towns of Cyprus from the copper mines, after partial smelting on the spot, where there was good supply of timber for the furnaces. The final smelting took place in workshops of the harbour towns, from which copper was exported in the form of oxhide ingots. Metallurgy and the export of copper formed the basis of the economy of Cyprus during the Late Bronze Age. It particularly flourished during the 12th century B.C.

Cyprus Museum, Nicosia, Enkomi no.1960 (Cyprus Department of Antiquities excavations).
Height: 26.3 cm.; diameter: 35 cm.

80

A bronze stand from Episkopi (Kourion). It consists of a ring supported on four cylindrical legs. On all four sides there are rectangular panels decorated in the *ajouré* technique. In each panel there is a human figure in front of a stylised 'sacred' tree: one holds an unidentifiable object on his shoulders, the second a fish, the third is seated, playing a lyre, and the fourth carries a copper ingot on his shoulders. Copper ingots were shaped like the hide of an ox, probably to facilitate their transport; they were of a standard weight. A fragmentary stand from the same period, which includes other scenes with an ingot-carrier, is now in the Royal Ontario Museum.

12th century B.C. British Museum, London, no.1920/12-20/1. Height: 11 cm.; diameter of ring: 8.5 cm.

81

A bronze stand, probably from Episkopi (Kourion). It consists of a ring, supported on four legs which are held together by means of eight cross-pieces. There is a ring at the lower terminal of each leg through which pass two axles for four wheels. The four sides of the stand are identically decorated with a panel in the *ajouré* technique, filled with animals in three rows; in the upper row a lion fights a bull; in the middle row a bull charges a fleeing lion; in the lower row there is a griffin(?) and a bull in a charging attitude. Below each panel is a bird-shaped pendant. Such stands were used as supports for lavers; reference to them is made both in the Bible and in the Homeric *Iliad*. There are several such stands, all found in Cyprus, dating to the 12th century B.C. Their *ajouré* decoration was probably influenced by ivory carving.

Cyprus Museum, Nicosia, no.1978/XI-21/1.
Height: 19 cm.

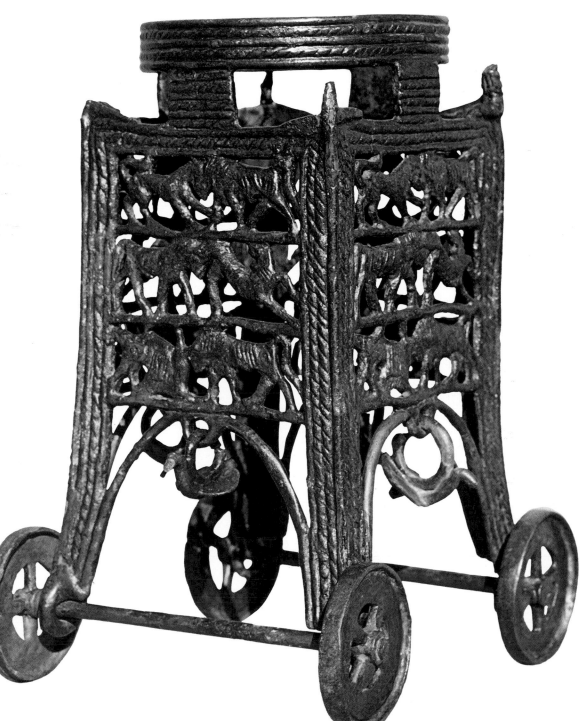

VI. THE END OF THE BRONZE AGE

Some time during the second quarter of the 11th century B.C., a natural phenomenon, probably an earthquake, destroyed the Late Bronze Age towns on Cyprus. Large portions of the mud brick superstructure of the Kition defensive wall tumbled down on the nearby street and much of the site at Enkomi was destroyed. Enkomi was not, of course, abandoned overnight. Some inhabitants remained behind, living as squatters in ruined houses. The sanctuary of the Ingot God continued functioning for some 25 years after the catastrophe. But by 1050 B.C. the old town was completely abandoned, and a new town called Salamis arose as a harbour centre whose importance is reflected in the wealth of the gifts found in an 11th century B.C. tomb which was excavated west of the harbour area.

At Kition, the population remained for about 50 years at the same sites, after rebuilding or repairing the ruined public buildings, but curiously not the city wall. In c. 1000 B.C., however, the inhabitants moved south, in order to be closer to the sea.

A town known as Palaepaphos was built on the ruins of the destroyed city and flourished for many centuries afterwards. In the meantime, new sites were chosen for Kourion and Lapithos not very far from the old ones. Soloi makes its appearance as a new town, at the site which developed as a major city-state during the historical period.

This also was a period of city-building, as recalled in the *nostoi*, the mythical stories connected with the return of heroes to their homes after the end of the Trojan War. According to tradition, some of the heroes did not return to their homelands but went to Cyprus. Teucer, the son of the king of the island of Salamis (near Athens), is said to have constructed a city near Cyprus' present-day Bay of Salamis which he named Salamis, after his own fatherland. He also introduced to the new city the cult of Zeus, built for him a sanctuary, and became the cult's first high priest.

Although Teucer's name was preserved at Salamis for about 1,000 years, as late as the 2nd century A.D., the story of his founding Salamis is believed to be a later invention, perhaps by the Athenians, as an attempt to justify their imperialist expansionist policies in the 5th century B.C. Nevertheless, in its broader aspect, the story does reflect a historical event — the last wave of Achaean colonisation, which finally Hellenised Cyprus by establishing for good the Greek language, religion and culture in the island. This is the conclusion of a long process of colonisation, which started more than 100 years earlier.

Before moving on to the most eventful aspect of this tumultuous period — the Iron Age — it would be prudent to examine the effect of Cypriot art on Greece itself. Though no Cypriot pottery has thus far been found in the Attica region, we have observed that a number of changes in its ceramic style occur between 1075 and 1050 B.C., both in shape and decoration. Bottles, ring vases and pilgrim flasks are innovations in sub-Mycenaean pottery which, according to a recently proposed theory, were introduced to Attica by Cypriots, or by Greeks who had settled in Cyprus and who, perhaps after the earthquakes of 1075 B.C., returned to Athens, taking with them these new styles.

82

Stirrup jar of Proto-Bichrome ware, from a
tomb at Alaas. It has a globular body, a false
neck with a knobbed top disc and air-hole
through the knob; a spout on the shoulder,
and two opposed handles. The shoulder is
decorated with five composite triangles. There
is a horizontal frieze of latticed lozenges
round the lower part of the shoulder;
horizontal bands round the body; transverse
strokes on the outer part of the handles, and
bands round the spout. The shape and the
decoration of this vase are Aegean and
particularly sub-Minoan. The pottery
decoration of this period (early 11th century
B.C.) is usually of one colour (black or dark
brown), but occasionally, as here, two
colours, black and purple, were used.

Cyprus Museum, Nicosia. Alaas,
Tomb 19, no.13. Height: 40 cm.

Kalathos (deep conical bowl with concave sides), from Palaepaphos. It is decorated in the Proto-Bichrome technique, both inside and out. The inside is divided into rectangular panels, some of which are filled with pictorial motifs: a goat and a human figure, a lyre-player, birds, a tree, and others with linear geometric motifs. The outside is decorated with linear geometric motifs in narrow panels and three broader panels, each containing an unidentifiable monster resembling a 'frog-man'. There is also a tree motif in another panel. The decoration of this vase is very unusual. It shows influences both from the Near East and from the Aegean.

Cyprus Museum, Nicosia. Palaepaphos, Tomb 9, no.7. Height: 15 cm.: diameter: 22 cm.

Jug of Proto-White Painted-White Painted I
ware, from Palaepaphos. The vase has a
globular body, concave neck and a strainer at
the mouth in the form of a bearded human
face. The actual strainer is through the beard.
The shoulder is decorated with composite
triangles and groups of concentric segments;
there are groups of horizontal bands round
the body, and three horizontal parallel wavy
bands round the neck. This is one of two
identical jugs found in the necropolis of
Palaepaphos-Skales. Such vases demonstrate
the sense of humour of the Cypriot potter
which is apparent from the Early Bronze Age
up to the Archaic period.

11th century B.C. Cyprus Museum, Nicosia.
Palaepaphos-Skales, Tomb 49, no.53.
Height: 26.6 cm.

85

Composite *kylix* (stemmed bowl) of Proto-Bichrome ware. The vase consists of three deep bowls, each with two opposed horizontal loop handles below the rim; they join one another and intercommunicate through three perforations. The bowls have a common stem with a flat splayed foot; there are two horizontal ridges round the stem. The decoration of each bowl consists of a horizontal chain of latticed lozenges on either side between the handles and a painted band at the rim; the stem is decorated with black paint. This is a unique form and illustrates again the inventive spirit and humour of the Cypriot potter.

Early 11th century B.C. Cyprus Museum, Nicosia. Palaepaphos - Skales, Tomb 67, no.53. Height: 15 cm.

VII. THE IRON AGE

The appearance of iron, like that of bronze and copper before it, was a revolutionary invention. When it came into widespread use the metal dramatically changed all aspects of life in the ancient world. Because it was much harder than bronze, iron rendered bronze obsolete, and gave those who possessed it, and had the means of fabricating it, unrivalled power and influence.

Iron oxide, like raw copper, was abundant on Cyprus, which meant that iron did not have to be imported. Ironworking was practised on a large scale c.1100 B.C., and was introduced to Greece by Greek settlers on Cyprus (iron pins and daggers of Cypriot origin were found in the Kerameikos tombs in Athens).

The invention of iron may be attributed to troubled conditions in the Eastern Mediterranean, which made sources of tin required for the production of tin-bronze inaccessible. The Cypriots, or perhaps the Achaean settlers with their advanced metallurgical skills, solved this problem by producing iron. Analysis of some of the Late Cypriot IIIB iron knives from Cyprus has demonstrated that Cypriots even produced a kind of steel — by carburizing and quench-hardening iron blades.

The early part of the Iron Age is also called Cypro-Geometric, because it is marked by a geometric style in pottery decoration. The Cypro-Geometric I period (c.1050-950 B.C.) is known only from artefacts found in tombs. Cemeteries from the Cypro-Geometric I period have been excavated at Lapithos, Kourion-Kaloriziki and, most recently, at Palaepaphos-Skales. At Lapithos, an interesting phenomenon is observed. There are two separate cemeteries: one for Greek immigrants, with chamber tombs in the Mycenaean style, and the other for the local indigenous population, where the traditional type of chamber tomb persists. The same ethnic separation may have pertained in the town itself, and shows that the two ethnic elements had not yet become completely integrated.

In three of the Lapithos tombs an unusual (for Cyprus) burial custom occurs —the sacrifice of slaves to serve their masters in an afterlife. At Kourion-Kaloriziki evidence has been found of incineration of the dead, a custom no doubt introduced by Greek immigrants. It should be mentioned here that there is no evidence for an early (12th century B.C.) Achaean colonisation of Kourion. Therefore, the Greeks must have come to this city during the last wave of colonisation, in the early 11th century B.C. It is these Greeks (Argives) whom Herodotus mentions as the ancestors of the Kourians.

Another interesting phenomenon observed in the necropolis at Kourion-Kaloriziki is the consistent orientation of the tombs, which is characteristic of Rhodian cemeteries of this period. It has been suggested that the Greek population of Kourion and other places where this occurs may have passed through Rhodes, where they remained for some time before coming to Cyprus. A Rhodian three-handled jar found in a Kaloriziki tomb supports this hypothesis. The necropolis of Kaloriziki also provided evidence for the social structure of the towns during this period.

The cemetery at Palaepaphos-Skales, about a mile southwest of the site of the temple of Aphrodite, is situated on the south slope of a hill. About four dozen tombs have been excavated there during recent years. The 11th century tombs (there are also some 10th and 9th century tombs and even some of later periods) have a consistent orientation like those at Kourion. They have large rock-cut chambers, and are more or less rectangular in plan, with a long narrow *dromos*. The chambers are 3 to 4 m. deep, and are carved in the soft rock, a fact which resulted in the collapse of almost all the chambers. This, however, had a positive effect too, as it sealed the tombs from looters.

The tombs were used for multiple burials. The skeletal remains from previous burials were usually put in one or more large amphorae together with all the valuable tomb gifts in order to make room for new burials. The tomb gifts are exceptionally rich, and include pottery in some very unusual shapes, both in Proto-White Painted ware, and in White Painted I. Cypro-Geometric I pottery is mostly decorated with geometric patterns, but there are pictorial elements as well: stylised fishes, birds and quadrupeds. Occasionally there are more ambitious compositions, such as the slaying of a large two-headed snake by two armed human figures, a composition which may illustrate a specific myth.

There are also imports from the Syro-Palestinian coast, in particular a number of flasks and juglets decorated with black paint on a red slip surface. Among the Syro-Palestinian imports the most popular are the "Canaanite" jars, a fact which indicates that by now the commercial relations with the Syro-Palestinian coast, which were close during the 14th and 13th centuries, have been renewed. This cultural interchange, in fact, may partly explain the wealth of 11th century Palaepaphos and Cyprus in general. We also found gold objects in abundance in the Palaepaphos tombs: a gold needle, ear-rings, finger-rings, gold diadems, as well as discs with embossed rosettes which adorned garments, and rectangular sheets of gold. Similar objects had been found in the tombs of Lapithos and were probably parts of tiaras or crowns. Other ornaments included D-shaped fibulae, most of them fabricated of bronze, but some also made of iron, and one made of silver decorated with gold beads. In addition, there were bronze pins with pomegranate-shaped heads — a type common in Greece from the 11th century onwards.

The Palaepaphos tombs were particularly rich in bronze vessels. Apart from the ordinary hemispherical bronze bowls, we found bowls with opposed loop handles, often topped by stylised lotus flowers. One of these large bowls has *protomes* of goats on the tops of its opposed loop handles. The most important of all the bronze vessels found up to now at Palaepaphos is a tripod cauldron of the sort that is well-known on the Greek mainland from the 12th century B.C. onwards, but which was found for the first time on Cyprus. This is indicative of the serious contribution of the Greek immigrants in metallurgical development.

In one of these tombs, a large stone scarab of Amenophis III was found. He was an Egyptian Pharaoh who lived more than 300 years earlier. The scarab has a long hieroglyphic text on its base, commemorating the exploits of the Pharaoh in lion-hunting. The presence of such scarabs, distributed among members of the Egyptian royal family, in a Cypriot tomb, leads to a number of fascinating speculations, including the possibility that a Cypriot married an Egyptian.

Another tomb discovery illustrates the high standard of living enjoyed by Greek aristocrats: a bath-tub carved out of limestone. (Clay bath-tubs were not unknown in the Aegean, e.g. at Pylos and Knossos, but they disappear by the 11th century during the period of poverty, which is known in Greece as the "dark ages").

In the tomb in which the bath-tub was discovered were three bronze skewers, of which one is engraved with five signs of the Cypriot syllabary. This was an exciting discovery because the symbols constitute the earliest known use of the Palaeopaphian syllabary, which succeeded the Cypro-Minoan script. The five signs represent the Greek proper name *Opheltes* in the genitive, in a type which is characteristic of the Arcadian dialect. The importance of this discovery cannot be overestimated. It constitutes the earliest evidence for the use of the Greek language in Cyprus, and what is equally important, of a dialect form which links it with Arcadia. According to mythical tradition the founder of Palaepaphos was Agapenor, the king of the Arcadians, who took part in the Trojan war. We know that there were special links between Palaepaphos and Tegea, the capital of Arcadia, even in later periods, and that at Tegea there was a temple of Aphrodite Paphia.

The Palaepaphos material demonstrates that the Greeks of Cyprus, unlike their kinspeople on the Greek mainland where there was illiteracy and poverty in the 11th century B.C., had formed prosperous communities which were trading with the Near East. Relations with the Aegean were not lacking either. Recent excavations at Lefkandi in Euboea have brought to light a number of Cypriot and Near Eastern objects. There is also Cypriot influence on the sub-Mycenaean pottery of Athens and Euboea. Whether these influences were the result of Cypriots trading with or visiting the Aegean, or whether the Euboeans had already found their way to the Eastern Mediterranean, as they did 150 years later, is not easy to determine.

The 10th and 9th centuries saw the complete fusion of the Greek and the indigenous Cypriot cultures, a process during which Cypriot styles often overwhelmed the Greek, as for example in funerary architecture. Relations with the Aegean were rather rare during this period and only the Euboeans sent some of their pottery to Cyprus; they received in exchange Cypriot pottery and bronzes. Cypriot objects also appeared in the Dodecanese. The closest relations, however, were with Crete. Cypriot pottery continued to influence Cretan pottery, a phenomenon which had already begun in the 11th century B.C. There were Cypriot objects in Crete, like bronze rod tripods, and the Cretans imitated in clay Cypriot bronze stands decorated in the cut-out technique.

A 10th-9th century B.C. bowl bearing an engraved Phoenician inscription is the earliest evidence we have found thus far of a contact with the Phoenicians. One may suggest that those responsible for the transport of Cypriot goods to Crete may have been Phoenician merchants. Such goods must have been the basis on which the Cretan orientalising style of the 8th century was founded. Recent excavations in the cemetery near Knossos have brought to light a large number of Cypriot slow-pouring flasks of Black-on-Red ware, and even local imitations of them. These must have contained perfume which was traded by the Phoenicians.

86
Gold sceptre from Kourion-Kaloriziki. It consists of a tubular shaft made of a thin sheet of gold, and topped by a globe decorated in *cloisonné* scale pattern. The cloisons were filled with white and blue enamel which has now turned a greenish colour. On the globe are two falcons, also decorated in the *cloisonné* technique. The gold shaft was probably fixed on to a longer shaft made of wood or ivory. This was probably the sceptre of a king, which symbolised royal authority. The *cloisonné* technique is rare for this period (early 11th century B.C.).

Cyprus Museum, Nicosia, no.199.
Height: 16.5 cm.

87

Bronze rod cast tripod with a pair of volutes at the top of each leg. The three legs support a flat ring which is decorated all round with a frieze of double spirals in relief. There are three outer struts, springing from about the middle of each leg and joining with the lower part of the ring. There are also three inner struts; they are joined to each leg at the level of the outer struts and to an inner ring. The legs consist of double rods. Within the loop of the outer struts, at the point where the struts join the ring, there are two rings for the suspension of pendants, which are missing. Such tripods were exported from Cyprus to the Aegean. They date from the 12th-11th century. B.C.

11th century B.C. Cyprus Museum, Nicosia. Palaepaphos-Skales, Tomb 58, no.31. Height: 30.3 cm.

88

Bronze bowl from Palaepaphos. Hemispherical body, with a plain rim, and a round base. It was probably cast and partly hammered afterwards. There are two horizontal parallel grooves on the outside below the rim; two opposed horizontal loop handles rivetted to the body through disc-shaped attachments; and two bridges of twisted wire between the handles and the body of the bowl. At the top of the handles there is a stylised lotus flower.

11th century B.C. Cyprus Museum, Nicosia. Palaepaphos-Skales, Tomb 58, no.90. Height: 8.1 cm.; diameter: 20.1 cm.

89

Large bronze bowl from Palaepaphos. It has a hemispherical body, with plain rim and round base; it was probably cast and then hammered. There are two opposed horizontal loop handles rivetted to the bowl; they are upcurved and are decorated at the top with protomes of goats; they are bridged to the body by means of twisted wire. Bronze bowls of the 11th century B.C. are usually small and handleless, but the Palaepaphos-Skales Cypro-Geometric cemetery has produced an extraordinary variety of large bowls. Metallurgy must have flourished in this area during the very beginning of the Iron Age.

Cyprus Museum, Nicosia. Palaepaphos-Skales, Tomb 49, no.1.
Height: 20 cm.; diameter: 37.1 cm.

90

Askos of White Painted I ware. It is in the
form of a 'stirrup jar', but with a basket handle
instead of the vertical opposed handles; on
the shoulder are two extra spouts, opposed to
one another, in the form of a bull and a
ram-protome respectively. The same cemetery
produced other animal-and bird-shaped askoi.

11th century B.C. Cyprus Museum, Nicosia.
Palaepaphos-Skales, Tomb 76, no.114.
Height: 21.5 cm.

91

Gold rectangular plate with folded edges. It is
decorated with an embossed figure walking to
right, with a flower or bough in both hands.
The figure wears a crown or tiara; its long
locks of hair fall at the back of the shoulders.
It wears a long robe, decorated with a
'guilloche' pattern along the border. Four
other identical plates were found in the same
tomb. They probably formed part of a crown,
with joined plates, like the one the female
figure on the plaque is wearing. The plates
were joined with wires of bronze which are
still preserved in the folded edges of each
plate.

10th-9th century B.C. Cyprus Museum, Nicosia.
Palaepaphos-Skales, Tomb 67, no.8.
Height: 9.4 cm.

92

An engraved inscription on a bronze skewer
(*obelos*) from Palaepaphos. Skewers, made of
bronze or iron, appear among the tomb-gifts
of warriors from the 11th century B.C.
onwards, as prestige objects. Homer in the
Iliad often refers to the meal of heroes which
consists of meat roasted on skewers. The
skewer of which this is a detail was found
together with two others in a rich tomb at
Palaepaphos. The engraved inscription, in the
Palaeopaphian syllabic script, represents a
Greek name in a genitive form which is
particular to the Arcadian dialect: *Opheltau*
(= of Opheltes). This is the earliest evidence
which we have (11th century B.C.) for the use
of the Greek language. We know that
according to mythical tradition the founder of
Palaepaphos was Agapenor, king of the
Arcadians, who came to Cyprus after the end
of the Trojan war.

Cyprus Museum, Nicosia. Palaepaphos-Skales,
Tomb 49. Length: 87.2 cm.

VIII. NEW TEMPLES AND DEITIES: THE PHOENICIAN INFLUENCE

The Phoenicians for the most part relied on trade and trading outposts to make their presence felt, not just in Cyprus, but all over the Mediterranean. Inexhaustible sailors and traders, they even ventured as far west as North Africa, where they founded a city that later expanded into a powerful nation.

The Phoenician presence was a relatively new phenomenon in Cyprus, however, for though relations between Cyprus and the Syro-Palestinian coast had been very close since the Late Bronze Age, it is only from the middle of the 9th century B.C. onwards that one may speak of a Phoenician influence on Cyprus. The Phoenicians first set foot on Cyprus during their westward expansion. They sailed from their city-state at Tyre (the modern Lebanese city still bears this name) and reached Kition, on the south-east coast of the island.

Recent excavations have revealed the size and importance of the Phoenician presence in this coastal town. The Phoenicians built two important sanctuaries here, one for the god Heracles-Melqart near the harbour and the other for Astarte, the Phoenician goddess of fertility and love, on the foundations of the old Late Bronze Age Temple 1, which had been abandoned 150 years earlier.

The temple of Astarte is the most important structure, since the worship of this goddess had been instituted as the official cult of the Phoenicians. The ground plan of the original Late Bronze Age temple was kept and the holy of holies remained the same. But the courtyard was modified. The passage along the south side was abolished and the rectangle formed a courtyard with two spacious porticos along the north and south sides respectively. The roofs of the porticos were each supported by two parallel rows of wooden pillars, of which the stone bases, with rectangular sockets at the upper part to receive the wooden pillars, have survived. On either side of the central entrance to the holy of holies were two free-standing rectangular pillars built of ashlar blocks. These resemble the biblical columns of Jachin and Boaz (which are described as being of bronze) in the temple of Solomon in Jerusalem — which was also built by Tyrian masons.

An inscribed Phoenician bowl was found on the earliest floor of the temple of Astarte. The inscription refers to a sacrifice to Astarte by a Phoenician who went from Tamassos to Kition, prayed to Astarte, and sacrificed in her honour. Then he had his hair cut, put it in that very bowl, and dedicated it to the goddess. We know this custom from Lucian, a later Greek author. He mentioned that at Hierapolis in Syria he performed the same ritual when he was a young man. It is interesting to note that a 4th century B.C. inscription, found at the end of the 19th century at Kition and now in the British Museum, lists among the personnel of the temple of Astarte, sacred barbers who performed ritual haircuts.

Of the other smaller Late Bronze Age temples in the same area, Temple 2 was demolished and its place was occupied by a large rectangular courtyard with an altar, which served the main temple; Temples 4 and 5 were restored on a smaller scale. The discovery of Greek Geometric pottery on the floor of Temple 5 helps date the temple on the one hand, and demonstrates, on the other hand, that intercourse with the Aegean was resumed, even in a city dominated by the Phoenicians, a people considered hostile to the Greeks. The reason for this detente may have been the same then as it is today: when it comes to trade and profit, ethnic prejudices become problems of secondary importance.

The Phoenicians called Kition *Qarthadast* (New Town), the same name which was given later to Carthage. By the middle of the 9th century B.C. the Phoenicians probably had political control of Kition, but their influence must have extended far beyond this town. The fact that a Phoenician is said to be an inhabitant of Tamassos, a copper producing area, is significant. The copper ores of Cyprus as well as its timber (for smelting and ship-building) were undoubtedly the two commodities which attracted this seafaring nation of traders. Their influence

is also seen at Amathus, west of Kition, where recent excavations of tombs have brought up a rich collection of Phoenician artefacts.

By c. 800 B.C., the first Phoenician temple was destroyed by fire and was restored immediately afterwards. The wooden pillars of the porticos were replaced by two rows of masonry pillars. A sacrifice was performed in the south-western corner of the courtyard, and a foundation deposit of small jugs and bowls has been found near the sacrificial ashes. The offering was meant to assure the goddess that the reconstructed temple would not meet the same fate as the first one.

Another Cypriot sanctuary had a history similar to that of the one at Kition. This was the temple of Aphrodite of Palaepaphos. It is only in the 4th century B.C., however, that one finds the earliest reference to it in an inscription, as the temple of Astarte Paphia. But the material which has been discovered in the area of the temple, at least from the Archaic period, is of strong Phoenician character. Representations of Astarte in terracotta are numerous. Even the goddess with uplifted arms, which was introduced from Crete, is now transformed and adapted to the Astarte type: she retains her tiara and her special facial characteristics, but like Astarte is depicted nude.

93

Fragmentary bowl of Red Slip ware, from the temple of Astarte at Kition. Its outer surface was engraved with an inscription in the Phoenician alphabet, of which only a part survives. It mentions an inhabitant of Tamassos (a copper mining centre in the central part of Cyprus), who went to Kition, prayed to Astarte, and offered sacrifices in the goddess' temple for himself and his family; then he cut his hair and dedicated it to the temple, having put it in that very bowl. This custom is known from other places and other periods, particularly in the Near East. The bowl was found on the first floor constructed in the temple and may be dated to the end of the 9th century B.C. The inscription helped to identify the divinity who was worshipped in the temple, though there is no general agreement among scholars about the interpretation of this inscription.

Cyprus Museum, Nicosia. Kition, Temple 1, no.1435. Height: 5.8 cm.; restored diameter: 25 cm.

94, 95

Two jugs of Red Slip Phoenician ware, found in the necropolis of Amathus. The small jug has a characteristic mushroom-like mouth and a carinated shoulder. The other jug has a conical neck and trefoil mouth. Such jugs are also known in bronze and silver throughout the Phoenician and Punic worlds. The introduction to Cyprus of both of these shapes influenced the Cypriot potter who reproduced them in a number of local Cypriot wares. Amathus was at an early stage under the cultural influence of the Phoenician colony at Kition.

8th century B.C. Limassol District Museum. Amathus Tombs 276 no.278 and 302 no. 52 respectively.
Height: 22 cm. and 25 cm. respectively.

96

A wall-bracket or incense-burner from the Famagusta District, decorated in the Bichrome III style. It consists of a flat plaque with a pointed top with a hole for suspension; at the lower part of the plaque there are two joined, semicylindrical projecting pieces with a horizontal brace across their tops. The central part of the plaque is decorated with a standing nude female figure in relief; its arms are prominently bent forward. It wears a tiara and has red spots on its cheeks, recalling the Cretan 'goddess with uplifted arms'. The body is decorated with linear geometric patterns like the rest of the surface of the plaque. Above the head of the female figure, near the top of the plaque, are two ox heads in high relief. This is the largest and one of the most elaborate wall-brackets ever found in Cyprus. Such objects are known in bronze but mainly in clay from the Late Bronze Age onwards. In the Late Bronze Age they are part of the furniture of sanctuaries.

9th-8th centuries B.C. Hadjiprodromou Collection, Famagusta. Height: 70 cm.; width: 25 cm.; depth: 14.5 cm.

97
Terracotta of a female figure decorated in the Bichrome technique. It represents the well-known 'goddess with uplifted arms' who was originally imported from Crete in the 11th century but survived in Cyprus up to the 5th century B.C., having been identified with the local goddess of fertility. It has a cylindrical body splayed at the lower part. The breasts are prominent, the eyes are swollen; the goddess wears a tiara, has red spots on her cheeks, and wears necklaces. The goddess is often represented as a nude woman (see no.92), and may represent the actual goddess or a priestess.

C.8th century B.C. Pierides Foundation Museum, Larnaca. Height: 23.5 cm.

IX. THE ARCHAIC PERIOD: INDEPENDENT KINGDOMS

The end of the Cypro-Geometric period is usually placed in the middle of the 8th century B.C. by archaeologists. These years were not marked by abrupt political or cultural change. Indeed, as has been attested to by new epigraphical evidence, the Phoenicians extended their influence. For instance, on two bronze bowls said to have been found near Limassol, there is an engraved inscription which clearly shows the religious ascendance of the Phoenicians. It reads:

"The Governor of Qarthadast [Kition], servant to Hiram [King Hiram II, who reigned during the third quarter of the 8th century], to Baal of Lebanon, his Lord".

Other bronze and silver bowls found in Cyprus and in other parts of the Mediterranean (Greece and Etruria) are decorated with engraved and *repoussé* patterns, mainly pictorial compositions with human and animal figures that include dances, and religious and hunting scenes. This style, usually called Cypro-Phoenician, may have originated in Cyprus under strong Phoenician influence and covers the period from the 9th to the 7th century B.C. The number of silver bowls increased considerably during the 8th and 7th centuries, the period when the Phoenicians, probably accompanied by Cypriots, traded along the Spanish coast, where they probably obtained the silver.

In other aspects, however, the local Cypriot art developed along traditional lines, though it was enriched, especially in its iconography, by the infusion of Phoenician ideas. In vase-painting, the pictorial style developed even further, often under the influence of the engraved metal bowls. Other influences were tapestries and embroideries.

The end of the 8th century was marked by a major political event that had a profound effect on Cyprus — the rise of the Assyrians as a new political power in the Near East. In 707 B.C., the Assyrian king Sargon II subdued seven Cypriot kings, an event he boastfully recorded on a stele which was erected at Kition, and in other inscriptions in the palace of Khorsabad in Assyria. The names of these kings, who also paid tribute to him in gold, silver and valuable furniture, are not mentioned. But in a later inscription, on the prism of Esarhaddon (673/2 B.C.), which commemorates the rebuilding of the Assyrian palace of Nineveh, 10 kingdoms "in the land of Iatnana [Cyprus], in the middle of the sea", are listed as being forced to pay tribute. These Cypriot Kingdoms were: Qarthadast, Idalion, Chytroi, Paphos, Kourion, Tamassos, Ledroi, Salamis, Soloi and Nure (Amathus?).

Assyrian rule was lenient, however, since the various kingdoms on the island were allowed to remain independent, as long as they paid regular tribute to the Assyrian king. This period in fact marked the apogee of the island kingdoms' development. Political, social, and cultural life developed round the palace, with the king as godhead. And since the king was also the religious leader in each city, he organised festivals, during which bards sang epic poems like the "Cypria", which was written by the Cypriot poet Stasinos.

The wealth of the kings and their pompous way of life is reflected in the splendour of the royal tombs of Salamis. These tombs, which may also have served nobles and even wealthy citizens, are mostly dated from the end of the 8th century B.C. to the beginning of the 7th century B.C. — a period which corresponds to the early years of Assyrian rule. The tombs consist of rock-hewn chambers with long broad *dromoi* in front of them. In most cases these chambers had been looted, but important finds were made in the *dromoi*, including the skeletons of sacrificed horses, and richly ornate chariots — a burial custom which is often characterised as "Homeric".

Other Homeric features in the royal tombs include the sacrifice of slaves to serve their masters in an afterlife, and the offering of amphorae filled with olive oil (one vase has a painted inscription under the handle reading: "Of olive oil"). Furniture made of wood and ivory, found in Tomb 79, corresponds very closely to Homer's description of Penelope's throne and Odysseus' bed.

The ivory bed and throne are decorated with exquisite plaques, carved either in relief or in the cut-out (*ajourée*) technique, in an Egyptianised Phoenician style. Both stylistically and technically (the use of thin sheets of gold or paste inlays) they recall the famous ivory furniture found in the palace of Nimrud in north Syria. The Salamis ivories may, in fact, have been made in one of the Syrian workshops and may have been sold by the Phoenicians to the court of Salamis.

One of the most spectacular objects found in the *dromos* of Tomb 79 is a large bronze cauldron, made of two beaten sheets of bronze. Its rim is decorated with rivetted accessories, eight cast griffin *protomes* and four beaten Janus-headed bearded sirens. The cauldron is supported by an iron tripod. Such cauldrons are known from Delphi, Olympia, and, Etruria, but it was the first time that one had been found in the Eastern Mediterranean.

Sacrificed horses found in the *dromoi* of tombs at Tamassos and Palaepaphos are also associated with other gifts which mark the high rank of the deceased: iron skewers and iron fire-dogs like those found in tombs of warriors in Greece, e.g. at Argos in the Peloponnese. A bundle of 12 skewers was discovered in Tomb 79, together with a pair of fire-dogs which have the form of a stylised warship.

Inhumation was usually practiced in the royal tombs of Salamis, but in two cases there is evidence of incineration. In Tomb 1, the carbonised skeletal remains of a woman were found in a large bronze cauldron. Among the ashes was a gold necklace and rock-crystal beads. These belonged to a Greek "princess" who probably married a member of the royal family of Salamis. She brought with her "dowery" of vessels from Greece, a large crater and an entire set of bowls and dishes. The latter constitute the largest group of Middle Geometric bowls and sub-Protogeometric plates thus far found in a single tomb in Cyprus. Several such imported vases, particularly

drinking cups, have been found in the recently excavated tombs of Amathus. No doubt the continuous contacts of the Euboeans with their Eastern Mediterranean colonies (Tarsus in Cilicia and Al Mina in north Syria) strengthened relations between Cyprus and the Aegean. It has been suggested that the Euboeans were accompanied by Cypriots when they started their colonial expansion in the East.

In the *dromos* of Tomb 3, which was covered by a *tumulus* of earth, the weapons of a 7th century B.C. warrior were found next to a war chariot. They consist of a spear, a shield, a bow, a quiver and an iron sword 91 cm. long with silver-plated rivets. The sword is intriguing as it corresponds to the much discussed "silver-studded" sword often referred to by Homer. Scholars have suggested that the Homeric features in the Salamis tombs may have been the result of a revival of the Homeric epic in the royal court of Salamis.

Also noteworthy among the objects found in the *dromoi* of the royal tombs are the bronze equestrian gear and chariot accessories, often decorated in *repoussé* with compositions taken from Oriental repertory. These constitute the *koene* style, which is a stylistic and iconographic admixture of Phoenician, Assyrian and Urartian elements, made by "international" craftsmen of the Eastern Mediterranean. It is not improbable that the bronzes were made by these artists on Cyprus, where copper was plentiful.

While the so-called "royal" tombs of Salamis were reserved for royalty and wealthy aristocrats, ordinary Salaminians were buried in a separate cemetery, in rock-cut chamber tombs with stepped *dromoi*. The most important of these tombs imitated burial customs used in the royal tombs — e.g., the sacrifice of a slave or a mule. Greek vases and local imitations, particularly drinking cups and storage amphorae from Attica, have been found in these tombs.

A noteworthy burial custom associated with this part of the Salamis cemetery is the occurrence of funerary pyres. Remains of a number of these have been found near the surface in the proximity of the funerary chambers. They consist of shallow pits in which bloodless sacrifices and libations were offered in honour of the dead. Such pyres were also a common feature in the Greek world.

The 7th century B.C. was a period of prosperity and artistic development. The Salamis "royal" tombs offer but a glimpse of the wealth of the kings, as one may imagine from the luxury of their palaces. When the Assyrian empire began to break up in 669 B.C., the Cypriot kings were more free to exercise their own cultural policies. They communicated often with the main centres of the Hellenic world, especially Delphi, where they dedicated gifts to the sanctuary of Apollo. Cypriot objects, including bronzes, terracottas and limestone statues, have been found in the temple of Hera at Samos. In fact, the Mainland Greeks developed a taste for Cypriot art, no doubt because of its originality and liveliness. In the meantime, Cypriot artists travelled widely. In the Greek colony of Naucratis in Egypt as well as in Samos and Rhodes, there is evidence that Cypriot artists produced minor sculpture in limestone.

Vase-painting also flourished during this period. The predominant decoration was Bichrome, with a predilection for the pictorial style. The rigidity of the Cypro-Geometric style was abandoned, and vase-painters decorated the curved surfaces of their vases with freely-drawn pictorial motifs, (bulls, birds, fishes, etc.) on a white background. This is called the "free-field" style because the pictorial motifs are freely applied on an empty surface without having to be adapted to any other decoration on the same vase, as was the case during the Geometric period.

The period of political stability enforced by the Assyrians — a stability that fostered the production of art — was disrupted when the Egyptians replaced the Assyrians in the hegemony of the Near East in 570 B.C. The Egyptian Pharaoh Amasis conquered Cyprus and ruthlessly oppressed its inhabitants. Artists opposed Egyptian influences by developing Greek artistic styles, particularly in sculpture, which competed with the Egyptian styles of their masters.

A striking example of this is found in monumental Cypriot sculptures, where one observes the rigidity, even the dress, of Egyptian statues, and the Ionic influence, especially in the use of naturalistic facial expressions, is often apparent too.

The antagonism between Oriental and Greek life-styles was at the expense of the indigenous Cypriot culture, which in the end was ousted in favour of the classical Greek culture.

The artistic ferment and the radical cultural innovations it spawned, however, are obvious only in Cyprus' major urban centres. Those living in the Cypriot countryside remained deeply rooted in ancestral traditions. Their conservative spirit finds its highest expression in the rural sanctuaries which have been found throughout the island. The small rural settlements did not worship specialised gods, but divinities who combined many different qualities, such as healing, fertility, protecting the worshippers in time of war, and against human and natural elements.

Apart from the usual sacrifices, worshippers reminded these gods of their piety and prayer through clay and stone statues or statuettes dedicated in the sanctuaries, their size depending on the financial means of those who dedicated them. There are statuettes in the image of the worshipper, holding a dove or a lamb, a permanent reminder of his gift to the god. Terracotta musicians were fashioned for the permanent satisfaction of the divinity. Soldiers departing for war dedicated an image of themselves fully armed in their war chariots, or in a boat — all to invoke the protection of a favourite god. Whenever sheltered benches in a sanctuary were full to capacity, these offerings were carefully set aside by priests, who would keep the valuable objects and bury "discards" in shallow pits in the vicinity of the sanctuaries known as *bothroi*. The discovery of such *bothroi*, which were the equivalent of rubbish pits, is a delight for the archaeologist.

A characteristic rural sanctuary was excavated by members of the Swedish Cyprus Expedition at the village of Ayia Irini, near the north-west coast. The sanctuary consisted of an enclosure with a boundary wall of rubble within which there was an open courtyard containing an altar, two small rectangular enclosures for sacred trees, and two shelters, of which only the stone sockets for the poles have survived. The sanctuary was in use from the Late Bronze Age until c. 500 B.C. It began as a sanctuary honouring a fertility divinity (symbolised by bulls and centaurs) and remained so throughout its long life. Votive offerings were arranged round the altar, while on the altar itself was a smooth oval stone that embodied the power of the divinity. This arrangement also occurs in other Cypriot sanctuaries and is perhaps a relic of a primitive prehistoric religion. One of the terracotta statuettes is of a human figure represented wearing a bull's mask, obviously a survival from a Late Bronze Age religious custom.

Next to some of these primitive sanctuaries are more advanced religious structures. One such sanctuary is at Meniko, a site west of Nicosia, and not too far from the copper mines near Tamassos. The Meniko sanctuary, dated to the late 6th century B.C., is situated near a river in the middle of cultivated land, and belonged to a community of farmers and shepherds, people whose ancestors inhabit this area today.

The divinity worshipped in this sanctuary was of course associated with fertility and cattle. But unlike the anonymous god of the Ayia Irini sanctuary, here one has a god who has been identified. He is Baal Amman, a Phoenician god who was known throughout the Phoenician world. To find a Phoenician deity in this particular Cypriot countryside is not unusual, as the Phoenicians had made their way to the Tamassos mining area by the 9th century B.C.

The sanctuary consists of two distinct architectural unities, each provided with a cella and a vestibule, entered through a staircase with a courtyard in front of it where traces of a sacrificial altar have been found. The courtyard was surrounded by a boundary wall. There was also a smaller rectangular structure for a sacred tree and two spare rooms for offerings. In the largest of the two cellas, a terracotta statuette of the bearded god Baal Amman was found. The god has characteristic ram's horns, wears a long robe, and is seated on a throne. Several incense-burners were found in the same cella. This is significant, as Baal Amman means "the god of the incense-burners". This is the first time that the god was found in a sanctuary with his attributes.

In the second cella a large limestone slab was found, carved in the shape of the "horns of consecration". This is the symbol of the goddess Tanit, who is known in the Punic pantheon as Baal Amman's companion. The Tanit discovery is significant because it indicates that two Phoenician divinities were worshipped — although these divinities were assimilated with traditional divinities of fertility, which had been worshipped in Cyprus since the Bronze Age.

Another sanctuary from the same period was excavated in Limassol. The divinity worshipped in the sanctuary was also a divinity of fertility — a fact illustrated by the inclusion of several clay figurines of a phallic character used for offerings. Also found were numerous clay zoomorphic vases representing bulls with genitals prominently showing, and a clay phallus.

While old religious beliefs and traditional offerings to the divinity of fertility were commonplace in rural sanctuaries, the situation was quite different in urban centres. By the end of the 6th and the beginning of the 5th century B.C., the Greek gods and goddesses were worshipped alongside local divinities. In the sanctuary of Apollo at Potamia, which is in the central part of the island near Idalion, Apollo is represented by large limestone statues. At Kition there is a sanctuary to Heracles-Melqart where limestone sculptures of this hero, worshipped in Cyprus as a god, were found. There was also a small limestone statue of Zeus Keraunios (the Thunderer). A sanctuary of Aphrodite was found west of Salamis, along with numerous limestone statuettes of the goddess. Most of them represent a female figure or "kore", draped in the fashion of the marble "korae" found at the Acropolis in Athens. There was a temple of Athena on the Acropolis at Idalion and a temple of Apollo of the Woods existed at Kourion from the 8th century B.C. onwards. Recent excavations have revealed its archaic altar, with offerings of gold, silver and clay figurines.

The dead kings and nobles continued to be buried with great pomp in monumental tombs during the late Archaic period. The "royal" tombs of Tamassos, with their carved interior decorations, are good examples of funerary architecture at the end of the 6th century B.C. Of the two tombs which survive, one consists of a stepped *dromos*, an antechamber and a main chamber with a large stone sarcophagus. The "saddle" roof is made of stone "beams" carved in relief on a stone slab in imitation of wooden architecture known from Anatolia. In fact, it is quite probable that itinerant Anatolian masons built this tomb, or instructed Cypriot workmen.

The glut of artistic styles was accompanied by an Egyptian rule that proved to be of very brief duration. By 545 B.C., after a period of only some 15 years, the Egyptians were swept aside in the Eastern Mediterranean by the more powerful Persians, whose hegemony was recognised by the kings of Cyprus. At the beginning, Persian rule was lenient — as long as the Cypriot kings did not agitate for independence and were willing to provide Persia with ships whenever they needed them in order to expand their empire.

Although the Cypriots were once more dominated by a foreign power, this time they were in good company, as Ionia too formed part of the Persian empire. A common fate had brought these two regions closer together, especially in the cultural field, where the influence of Ionian sculpture on Cypriot sculpture was significant. Goods from Ionia and from the Aegean in general were often imported to Cypriot urban centres like Salamis, Amathus and Kition.

Cypriots, as well as Phoenicians living on Cyprus, developed a taste for Cypriot art, Greek jewellery and luxury goods in general imported from the Aegean. Women followed Greek fashion in dress and hairstyle, and imported perfume from Corinth in luxurious vials. Exquisite seals or signet rings have been found on Cyprus. They were executed in a very fine style by Greek engravers working for a Cypriot and Phoenician clientele. Cypriot sculptors copied mythological scenes from imported Attic black-figure vases and "transplanted" them as low relief carvings on a stone sarcophagus from Golgoi, which is in New York City's Metropolitan Museum of Art. The Amathus potters also copied compositions from imported Athenian vases, going so far as to copy the techniques used in Black-Figure vase painting.

There must have been considerable wealth in the island during this period. One notices not only a flourishing import trade of luxury goods from abroad, but also a quantity of finely wrought jewellery worn by women, as seen in representations on stone and terracotta sculpture. Bracelets imitating the Persian style with heads of animals at the terminals, spiral hair ornaments decorated in the same fashion, necklaces with granulated beads, like the famous necklace from Arsos, now at the Cyprus Museum — all these attest not only to considerable wealth but also to a high level of artistic skill.

Despite their vassalage, the kings of Cyprus appear to have enjoyed a high degree of independence. This was particularly true of the Salaminian king. By c. 530 B.C., he was casting his own silver coins, using as his emblem the ram (a Persian motif), and the *ankh*, which is the Egyptian symbol of good luck. This king Evelthon must have been an able diplomat, since according to Herodotus he was also sending gifts (a bronze incense-burner) to the sanctuary of Apollo at Delphi, a shrine sacred to Persia's major enemies, the Greeks.

98

Bronze cauldron supported on an iron tripod, from the 'royal' necropolis of Salamis. The cauldron is made of two hammered sheets of bronze, held together by rivets. It is decorated round the rim with eight griffin protomes and four double-faced sirens with bearded human heads and birds' bodies, rivetted all round the rim. There are no handles. The griffins were cast, the sirens were hammered. The iron tripod, with a double ring supported on three rod legs, is decorated with three single vertical rods, the top of each forming a lily above a palmette. This is the first time that such a cauldron was found in Cyprus. Similar cauldrons are from Etruria, Delphi and Olympia, but the ultimate origin of this type may be Near Eastern, perhaps Urartian. Cauldrons are mentioned by Homer as prize pieces.

End of the 8th century B.C. Salamis Tomb 79, no.202. Cyprus Museum, Nicosia.
Total height: 125 cm.

99

Bronze breast-plate of a horse, from the 'royal' necropolis of Salamis. It is crescent-shaped, and is decorated in *repoussé* with a frieze of winged human figures and monsters from Near Eastern mythology. The style of the iconography is a mixed one with Urartian and Phoenician elements. No doubt this, like other decorated bronze plaques found in the Salamis tombs, was made by artists who had established a style common throughout the Eastern Mediterranean during the end of the 8th century B.C. The back of the breast-plate must have been covered with a piece of cloth or leather, hence the perforations round the edges. The horses which were pulling the funerary hearse or the war-chariot of the deceased were richly decorated for the funerary ceremony.

End of the 8th century B.C. Salamis Tomb 79, no.164. Cyprus Museum, Nicosia. Height: 43 cm.

100

Bronze front band for a horse, from the 'royal' necropolis of Salamis. It consists of two plaques which are hinged together. There is a crest fixed near the top of the upper plate. Both plates are decorated in high *repoussé* with human and animal figures. At the upper plate there is a horizontal row of three *couchant* lions and another row of four *urei* (snakes). The lower plate is decorated with two rows of three standing human figures. Those on the upper row are bearded and wear short chitons and Egyptian head-dresses. Those on the lower register are nude, female, and wear Egyptian head-dresses. Near the hinge, above the heads of the male figures, there is a solar disc which was inlaid with paste, now missing. The lower part of the plate terminates in a voluted palmette.

End of the 8th century B.C. Salamis Tomb 79, no.190. Cyprus Museum, Nicosia. Length: 50 cm.

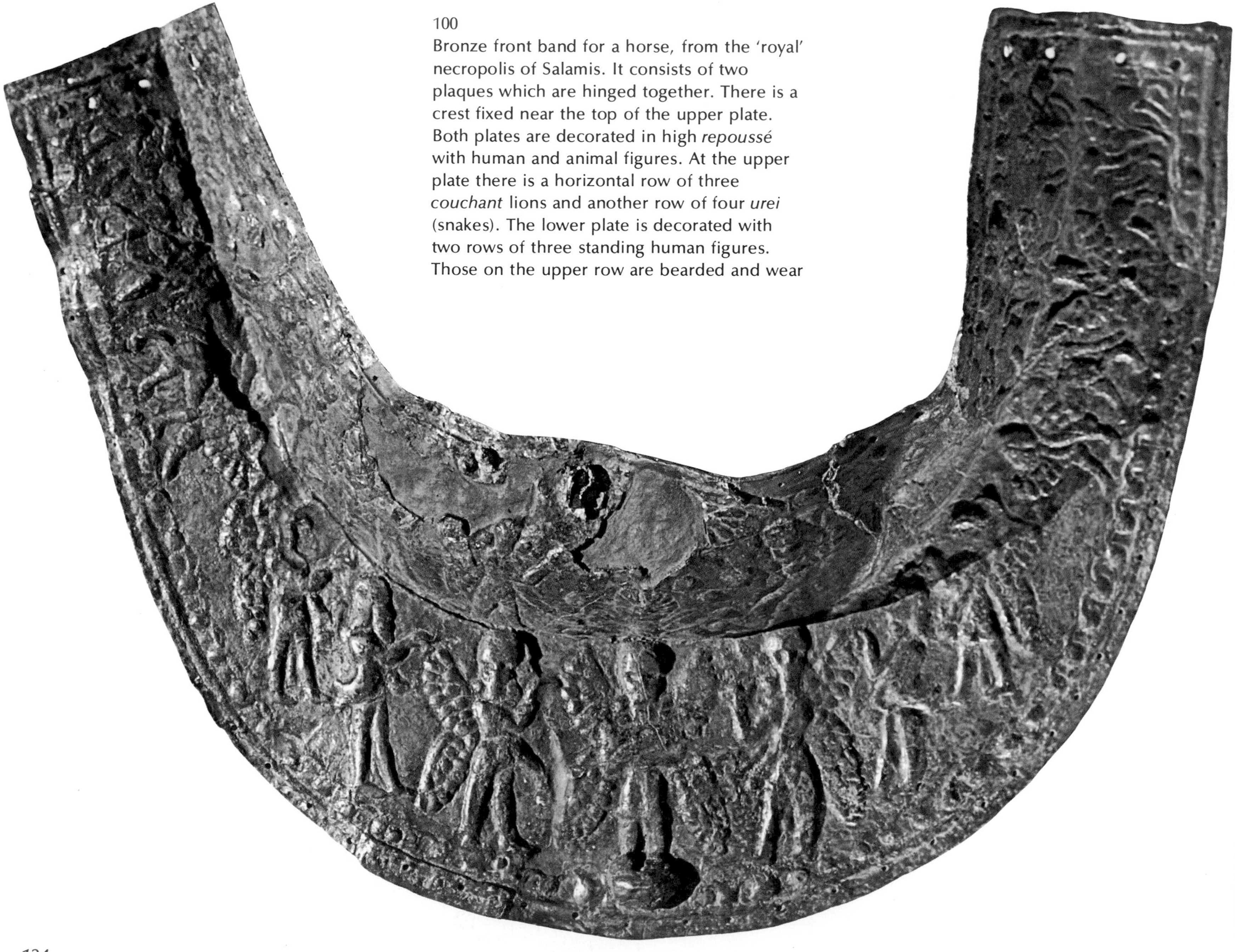

101
Bronze side pendant ornament for a horse, from the 'royal' necropolis at Salamis. It consists of a thin circular disc which is hinged to a narrow rectangular plate at the upper part; above it is a smaller plate, which is rounded at the top and hinged to the larger plate. The disc and the rectangular plate are decorated in *repoussé*. The central figure of the decoration of the disc is a nude winged female figure (Astarte), who stands on the back of two lions which turn their heads upwards; they hold a calf or a bull in their mouths. Astarte holds in each hand a lion by the hind leg. The lions are connected to a winged griffin. Above the head of the female figure is a winged Hathor's head. The rectangular plate is decorated with horizontal friezes of animals; there is also a frieze of animals round the perimeter of the circular disc. Such objects are often represented on horses on Assyrian stone reliefs.

End of the 8th century B.C. Salamis Tomb 79 nos.155 and 162. Cyprus Museum, Nicosia. Height: 58 cm.; diameter of disc: 29.5 cm.

102

Two ivory plaques from the 'royal' necropolis at Salamis. They formed part of the decoration of an ivory throne and were placed below the handles. They are carved on both sides in the *ajouré* technique and are inlaid with coloured paste. The thin walls of the inlaid depressions (*cloisons*) were covered with thin sheets of gold. At their upper and lower parts the plaques have tenons for fixing to the throne.

One of the plaques represents a composite stylised tree consisting of papyrus flowers and voluted palmettes, the other a winged sphinx wearing the crowns of Upper and Lower Egypt. Stemmed flowers spring from the lower tenon. The quality of the carving is very fine and can be compared with the best products of Near Eastern ivory carving, such as those found in the palace of Nimrud. The plaques

may have been made in a workshop in North Syria from which they were exported to Cyprus.

End of the 8th century B.C. Salamis Tomb 79, nos.143 and 258 respectively.
Cyprus Museum, Nicosia.
Height: 16.4 cm. and 16 cm. respectively.

103

A necklace of gold and rock-crystal beads found among the cremated remains of a 'princess' in a tomb of the 'royal' necropolis at Salamis. The necklace consists of six globular beads of rock-crystal, six gold-ribbed beads of globular depressed body and five cylindrical gold spacers. The cremated remains were found in a bronze cauldron which was covered with a thin cloth. The same tomb produced a large quantity of Greek Geometric pottery, hence the suggestion that this was a tomb of a Greek 'princess' who married a Cypriot prince or king of the court at Salamis.

End of the 8th century B.C. Salamis Tomb 1, no.76. Cyprus Museum, Nicosia.

104

Askos of Black-on-Red ware from Kourion. It
has an elliptical body, with two spouts at
either end; one of them terminates into the
head of a bull (?); the other is concave with a
horizontal ridge round the middle and
out-curved rim. A basket handle runs from the
back of the bull's head to the ridge of the
other spout. Four short legs are tucked below
the body. The entire surface of the askos is
decorated with concentric circles, groups of
parallel lines, lattice patterns, ladder patterns,
etc. Details of the face of the bull are
rendered with paint.

8th century B.C. British Museum, London
(British Museum Excavations, 1895), no.C904.
Height: 19 cm.

105

Jug of Bichrome IV ware. Ovoid body, short
concave neck, trefoil mouth, handle from rim
to shoulder. The largest part of the body is
decorated with a bull figure walking to left
and lowering its head to smell a stylised lotus
flower. Its stem springs from the hoof of the
bull's right foreleg. There is a large
multi-petalled rosette above the bull's body,
which is drawn in black outline and is filled
with purple paint. The head is reserved. The
dewlap is rendered with concentric segments;
at the upper part of the body there is a
reserved space with vertical parallel lines,
probably indicating the ribs; at the back of the
body a reserved space is filled with concentric
segments. This style, with pictorial
compositions applied on the white surface of
a vase, without any geometric accessories or
divisions of the body with bands, is called
'free-field' style and flourished particularly
during the Cypro-Archaic I and II periods. The
aim of the best painters was to adapt the form
of the decorative motif to the curved surface
of their vase, and they often succeeded
admirably.

7th century B.C. Cyprus Museum, Nicosia,
no.1951/I-2/9. From the Eastern part of Cyprus.
Height: 28 cm.

106

Large amphora of Bichrome IV ware. Ovoid depressed body, cylindrical neck, flat out-turned rim, two opposed handles from rim to shoulder. The two shoulder zones between the handles are decorated with two antithetic sphinxes on either side of a 'sacred tree' in the form of a stylised lotus flower. Below this decorated zone there is a horizontal zone of meanders encircling the body, and below it horizontal parallel bands and rings. The neck is decorated with chequers. The sphinx is a favoured pictorial motif in Cypro-Archaic vase-painting. It is of Near Eastern origin, but the occurrence of the meander in the decoration of this amphora points also to the Aegean as a source of inspiration for the Cypriot vase-painter.

7th century B.C.
Cyprus Museum, Nicosia, no.B2009.
Height: 47.5 cm.; mouth diameter: 25.5 cm.

107

Jar of Bichrome IV ware. Straight sides narrowing upwards, carinated shoulder, collar neck, two opposed raised horizontal loop handles on body. The two zones on either side between the handles are decorated with a frieze of hatched meanders. Above and below there is a horizontal frieze of *guilloche* pattern. Below each handle there is a stylised lotus flower.

7th century B.C. Pierides Foundation Museum, Larnaca. Height: 15.5 cm.

108
Jar of Bichrome V ware found in a tomb at Goudhi, south of Marion (Paphos District). It has a globular depressed body with two opposed vertical handles; the foot is missing. The two sides between the handles are decorated with animal figures rendered partly in outline and partly in silhouette. On one side is a bird, a lion and a bull; on the other side a wild boar and two dogs. Horizontal parallel bands encircle the body above and below the handles. The style of the figure drawing as well as the small ornaments in the background of the decorated zones very closely recall the style of Rhodian vase-painting of the end of the 7th century B.C.

Beginning of the 6th century B.C. Paphos District Museum no.2235. Preserved height: 29.5 cm.; mouth diameter: 22.3 cm.

109
Amphoriskos of White Painted V ware, from Amathus. Ovoid globular body, cylindrical neck, out-curved rim, two opposed horizontal loop handles on shoulder. The amphoriskos is decorated in what is known as the Amathus style. On the one side, between the handles, there is a horse and a rider to right and a human figure walking in front of the horse and looking backwards; stylised tree motifs are in the background. On the other side of the vase there are two antithetic sphinxes on either side of a 'sacred tree'. There are flower motifs underneath the handles, and the base is decorated with an engraved flower motif. The artist imitates the Black Figure style of Attica and even uses engraved lines to render the details on the silhouetted body of the figures. Such Black Figure Attic pottery has been found in fairly large numbers in the tombs of Amathus.

6th century B.C. Limassol District Museum. Amathus Tomb 251, no.8. Height: 13.5 cm.

110
Two bull figurines, one of gold, the other of silver, from the Archaic altar of the Sanctuary of Apollo at Kourion. Their legs, ears and horns were made separately and were attached. The details of the faces are indicated by grooves. Their style may suggest Anatolian influence of the late 8th-early 7th century B.C. The bull, as the symbol of the divinity of fertility, is often found among votive offerings in archaic sanctuaries. The altar produced a number of other bull figures in terracotta.

Cyprus Museum, Nicosia. Excavations by the American Mission at the temple of Apollo at Kourion, 1980.
Length of the gold bull: 4.9 cm.;
length of the silver bull (tail missing): 6.4 cm.

111
Necklace from Arsos consisting of 40 lentoid beads with granulated decoration and a cylindrical pendant of agate decorated with gold mountings on either side. The pendant is topped by a gold bee and two *urei* (snakes) wearing Egyptian crowns. Such necklaces are often represented in Cypriot sculpture worn by women.

7th century B.C. Cyprus Museum, Nicosia. Cyprus Museum excavations at the temple of Aphrodite, 1917, no.100. Length: 33 cm.; length of pendant: 4.5 cm.

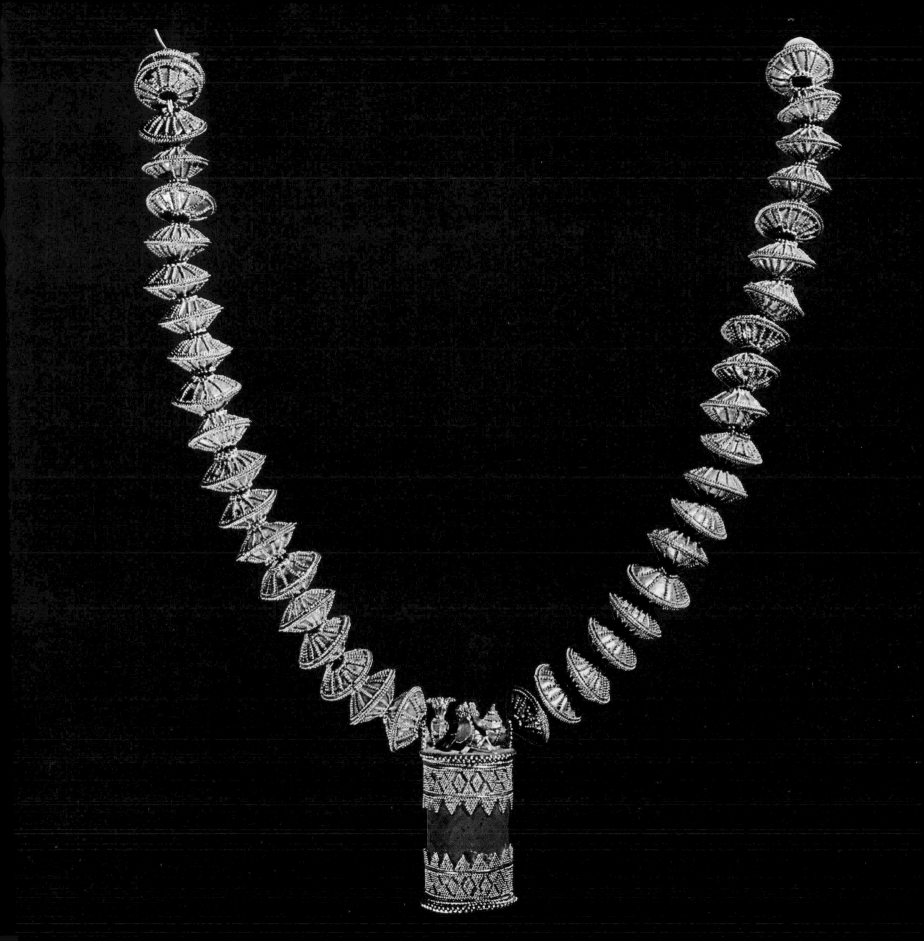

112
Drawings of the interior decoration of a built chamber tomb in the necropolis at Salamis (Tomb 80). The chamber was built of ashlar blocks and the painted decoration, in red and blue, was applied directly on the stone. The decoration on the sides consists of stylised long-stemmed lotus flowers and buds; the ceiling was decorated with star motifs, recalling the interior decoration of Egyptian wooden coffins. The tomb dates to about the middle of the 6th century B.C., i.e. the early years of the Egyptian domination of Cyprus.

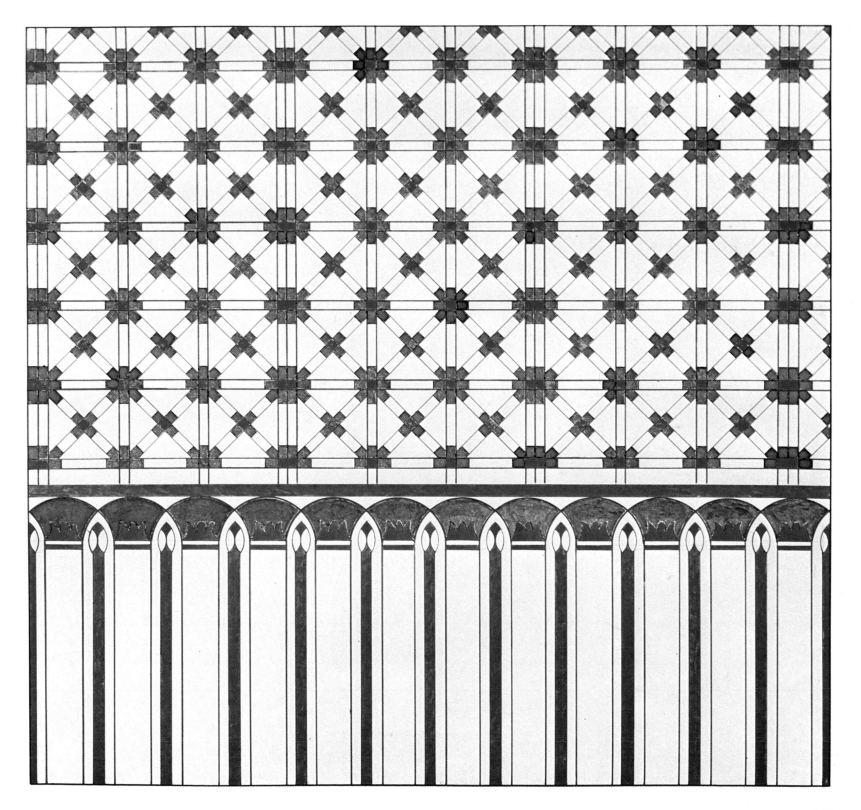

147

113
Terracotta figurine of a centaur or minotaur,
from the sanctuary of Ayia Irini. It has the
body of a bull, to which is attached the torso
of a human being. The head is bearded and
has bull's horns. The arms are stretched
forward. The sanctuary of Ayia Irini, near the
north-western coast of the island, produced a
large number of votive figures, such as bulls
and war-chariots, symbolising the qualities of
the divinity who was worshipped in the
sanctuary. There were also figures of
worshippers and several figures of minotaurs,
like the one shown here. They were probably
companions of the divinity. The combination
of a human torso with an animal body may
betray Greek influences.

C.600 B.C. Cyprus Museum, Nicosia. Ayia Irini
(excavations by the Swedish Cyprus
Expedition), no.1122.
Height: 28.1 cm.; length: 16.5 cm.

114

Terracotta figurine of a bearded Baal Hamman, seated on a throne, from a sanctuary at Meniko, west of Nicosia. The god wears a long robe. The sandaled feet rest on a stool. It has long coiling ram's horns, ram's ears, and a grave expression. Its face is painted red. Black and red paint is applied to the garments and the throne. Baal Hamman is a Phoenician and Punic god. In Cyprus the god is usually represented in limestone, and is seated on a throne which is supported by two rams. Found in the rural sanctuary of Meniko, dating to the 6th century B.C., the god was associated with the old Cypriot god of cattle and farmers, who was already known in the Late Bronze Age (see no.70).

Cyprus Museum, Nicosia. Meniko sanctuary no.1. Height: 18.5 cm.

115

A pair of terracotta incense-burners from the sanctuary of Baal-Hamman (no.114), at Meniko. Each consists of a hollow cylindrical stand topped by a detachable double bowl with lid, where the incense was burned. The upper part of the stands is decorated with a globe and drooping petals, in imitation of metallic incense-burners. Both stand and bowl are decorated with stripes of black and purple paint. The discovery of incense-burners in the sanctuary of Baal-Hamman is significant, since the name of this god denotes 'the god of the perfumed altar' (*hammanim* meaning incense-burner). There are several representations of the god, mainly on seals, seated on his throne in front of an incense-burner.

6th century B.C. Cyprus Museum, Nicosia. Meniko sanctuary nos.21, 26 & 33 and 22, 23 & 34 respectively.
Height: 38 cm. and 36.6 cm. respectively.

116

Terracotta figurine of a man wearing a bull's mask, from a tomb at Amathus. It has a cylindrical body splayed at the lower part; it holds the mask with both hands and is about to put it on its head. Both the mask and its body are decorated with stripes of black and purple paint. The custom of wearing bulls' masks during religious performances had a long tradition in Cypriot religion; we find it already at the end of the Early Bronze Age (no.31). In sanctuaries of the Late Bronze Age at Enkomi and Kition actual bulls' heads were found on the floors. The heads were used as masks by the priests or worshippers, who believed that by wearing a bull's mask they could acquire some of the qualities of the bull, which was the symbol of fertility and virility.

Cypro-Archaic II period. Limassol District Museum, Amathus Tomb 200, no.1.
Height: 13.2 cm.

117

Terracotta wall bracket from a tomb at
Amathus. It consists of a flat plaque against
which is moulded a standing female figure,
occupying almost the whole surface of the
plaque. At the top of the plaque there is a
hole for suspension; at the lower part is a
human arm at right angles with the plaque,
with a clenched fist and a perforation through
the fist, probably for the insertion of a
detachable stemmed lotus flower. A similar
wall-bracket in the Louvre shows the clenched
fist of the arm holding a detachable flower.
The human figure is draped, places both
hands below her breasts, wears ear-caps, and
has long hair that falls on either side of her
neck. Face and neck are painted red as well as
the projecting arm. Wall-brackets with nude
female figures in relief are known from slightly
earlier periods (no.96). Such objects may have
been used in sanctuaries of Astarte.

6th century B.C. Limassol District Museum.
Amathus Tomb 199, no.73. Height: 31 cm.

118
Two anthropomorphic masks, one protome of a female figure and one bull's mask, all of clay, found in tombs at the Amathus cemetery. One of the anthropomorphic masks has perforated eyes, the other does not. They are decorated with black and purple paint. Anthropomorphic and bulls' masks were worn during religious ceremonies, as already seen (see no.116) from the Early Bronze Age onwards. Miniature masks were often dedicated as votives. The Phoenicians were particularly fond of anthropomorphic masks, like the clay one below left of an apotropaic character.

6th century B.C. Limassol District Museum.
Height: from 8 cm. to 11.2 cm.

119

Clay model of a chariot, from a tomb in Larnaca. The chariot was drawn by four horses, of which one is now missing. There are two human figures in the chariot; one is large and bearded, the other a young boy. The chariot and the wheels are decorated with black, dark blue and purple paint; the spokes of the wheels are indicated both in relief and with paint. There is also paint on the horses; their blinkers are shown in white paint. This is one of the largest clay models of a chariot; they are usually found in sanctuaries, and are very rare in tombs.

6th-5th century B.C. Cyprus Museum, Nicosia. Larnaca, site 'Ayios Georghios', no.CS.2510/5. Height: 31.5 cm.

120

Five terracotta groups representing childbirth, from a 6th century B.C. sanctuary excavated at Lapithos in 1897. These terracottas were probably dedicated in honour of a mother-goddess who protected women in pregnancy. They are especially interesting in terms of the history of medicine; such primitive methods were used until some years ago among the country people of Cyprus.

Cyprus Museum, Nicosia, nos.B48,B54,B56,B65 and B55. Heights: from 8 cm. to 12.4 cm.

121
Terracotta figurine of a centaur. It has a
human head and torso and the body of a
quadruped (a bull ?). From its left shoulder
hangs a quiver, which may betray an
association with a war-god. We know that the
Greek centaurs were of a war-like nature. The
head is decorated with a crown of round
pellets, which allows a fringe of hair to appear
along the forehead. The facial characteristics
are rendered with black and purple paint. The
surface of the body is richly-decorated with
linear geometric motifs in black, purple and
light blue paint.

6th century B.C. Cyprus Museum, Nicosia,
no.1948/XI-29/1.
Height: 16.5 cm.; length: 11.5 cm.

122
Large terracotta head of a bearded figure,
from Tamassos. Hollow cast, with engraved
and painted hair, beard, eyebrows and
moustache. The large eyes are painted. The
figure must have been wearing a head-dress (a
turban?) now detached. The rectangular beard
is excessively large.

Proto-Cypriot style, end of the 7th century B.C.
British Museum, London, 1910.6-20.1.
Height: 36 cm.

X. WARS OF INDEPENDENCE

The Persians, like other rulers before them, did not administer Cyprus kindly for very long. The ambition of the Persian king was to conquer the Greeks in the Aegean so his fleet might dominate the Mediterranean. Since he recognised that a pro-Greek Cyprus would make this task even more difficult, by the end of the 6th century B.C., he was ruling Cyprus with an iron hand. He also encouraged antagonism among the 10 Cypriot kings, who accommodated him by dividing the island into pro-Greek and pro-Persian camps.

In 499/8 B.C. the cities of Ionia decided to revolt against the Persians, and the Greeks on Cyprus, inflamed by nationalist enthusiasm, followed their example. But the rebellion was soon crushed. Herodotus describes very vividly the various battles, the initial victories of the pro-Greek Cypriot kings, and also the betrayal of those who sided with the Persians.

For the next two centuries, the Cypriots fought to free themselves from the Persian yoke. But the Phoenician element in Cyprus and the attitude of those Cypriot kings whose ambitious policies caused them to align themselves with the Persian rulers, made the task of freeing Cyprus an almost impossible one.

The situation was exacerbated by the great distance between Athens and Cyprus, which left the Cypriots with little more than well-meaning moral support in their struggle for independence. Nonetheless, a renewed effort was mounted by Evagoras I, the great king of Salamis, to free the island from foreign domination. A consummate military man, Evagoras began a systematic campaign to wrest control of the island from the Persians. First the cities of the north and then those of the south fell to his soldiers. He captured Kition, the last stronghold of Persian influence on Cyprus. Then he turned outward: Tyre and several other Phoenician cities were subdued.

A descendant of the Teucrid family that founded Salamis, Evagoras was an inspired leader and an enthusiast of Greek ideals and culture who was highly praised by the Greek orator

Isocrates. During his eventful reign (411-374 B.C.), a large number of Greeks settled in Salamis, as they considered the rule of this king to be more benevolent than that of their own rulers. Certainly Salamis was a more cosmopolitan city than most. It was, in fact, second only to Athens among the wealthy and cultivated cities of the Mediterranean, and under Evagoras, the city-state prospered as never before.

But this enlightened king, who espoused a pan-Hellenic union of all Greeks under Athenian leadership, was to meet a tragic end. His initial successes were thwarted by the Persians, who sent an overwhelming force to Cyprus and forced Evagoras back to Salamis, where he was obliged to pay tribute to his conquerors. He was assassinated six years later.

If the pro-Greek kings were unable to defeat the Persians on the battlefield, they were successful in the field of culture. Never before had Cyprus been so "Greek". Greek artists were working on the island, thus keeping the local artists continuously informed of artistic developments on the Greek Mainland. The results were often spectacular. For example, some early 5th century B.C. limestone statues in the so-called archaic Cypro-Greek syle demonstrate that Cypriot sculptors could excel even when they worked in soft limestone, a material which is not suitable for sculpture.

An important monument emerged from this period of ferment — a fortress-palace, built on the north coast near Morphou Bay, by the pro-Persian king of Marion. The structure was sited on a hill so its inhabitants could watch supporters of the rebellious pro-Greek king of Soloi. Apart from the royal apartments, kitchens and so on, the palace was equipped in the fashion of Minoan-Mycenaean palaces with a series of storerooms. When the Greeks won a short-lived victory over the Persians and liberated Marion, the new pro-Greek king of the city had his revenge by changing the central part of the royal apartments so they looked like a *megaron*, which is a purely Greek architectural feature.

The Hellenisation of Cyprus also extended to the religious realm; Greek gods and heroes are enthroned in the Cypriot pantheon, thus accelerating a process that had started at the end of the 6th century. In a remote sanctuary at Kakopetria, on the north slopes of the Troodos mountains, the goddess Athena, the Athenian goddess par exellence, was worshipped alongside Heracles, the pro-Hellenic hero. Though her representations in terracotta or limestone are crude, it is nevertheless moving to witness how deeply the Greek gods were established in the religious feelings of the Cypriots, even in remote mountainous villages.

Greek artists were commissioned to prepare dies for the coins used by Cypriot kingdoms. These coins do not differ from those struck in other Greek cities except that the legends are in the Cypriot syllabary (and occasionally in the Phoenician alphabet, as for example on the coins of Kition). Greek deities like Athena, Apollo, Aphrodite and Heracles decorate their obverse sides.

123
Limestone head, slightly over life-size. It
represents a bearded youth, wearing a crown
decorated with rosettes. The hair is curly and
falls in a mass at the back of the head; there is
a fringe above the forehead. The beard and
the moustache are grooved for decorative
purposes rather than for naturalism. The smile
betrays influences of archaic Greek sculpture.

C.500 B.C. Cyprus Museum, Nicosia,
no.1968/V-30/696. Height: 32.5 cm.

124
Limestone statue of Zeus Keraunios (the
Thunderer), from Kition. The god has a
well-trimmed stylised beard and curly hair, the
mass of which falls at the back on the
shoulders. His smile (red-painted lips) betrays
influences of Greek sculpture. He wears a
mantle (*aegis*) and a long tunic. He is shown
striding forward (the feet are missing); his
right arm is bent upwards, with the
thunderbolt in his hand (now broken); his left
arm is bent forward and in the right hand he
clutched an eagle, of which only the claws
survive.

C.500 B.C. Cyprus Museum, Nicosia, Kition
Excavations of the Swedish Cyprus Expedition
on the 'Acropolis' of Kition (temple of
Heracles), no.139. Height: 56 cm.

125

Bronze slightly over life-size head of Apollo, from Tamassos, known as *the Chatsworth head*. The god has a severe expression. The rich hair was separately cast; it falls in curls on either side of the face, while two locks are tied above the forehead. This is no doubt the work of a Greek artist; it may well compare with the sculptures of the temple of Zeus at Olympia and may be dated to c.460 B.C. It is said that the complete statue of Apollo was found at Tamassos in 1836, and the head was broken off for export. It reached Smyrna and from there it was bought by Lord Chatsworth, and finally reached the British Museum.

British Museum, London, no.1958, 4-18, 1. Height: 31.6 cm.

126

Slightly over life-size head of limestone, from the sanctuary of Apollo at Potamia, near Idalion. The expression of the face reveals the influence of Greek sculpture at the end of the 5th century B.C. Although the facial characteristics are idealised, there are some features which suggest individual characteristics, such as the lips and chin. The hair is rendered in an archaistic manner, with a row of curls round the upper part of the forehead, and is crowned with a wreath. The sanctuary in which this head was found has been identified as a sanctuary of Apollo and this head may represent the god.

Cyprus Museum, Nicosia. Excavations of the Cyprus Department of Antiquities at Potamia (1933), no.55. Height: 30 cm.

127

Aerial view of the palace of Vouni, on the north-western coast of Cyprus. It was built in the 5th century B.C. by the king of Marion as the seat of a prince and as a garrison to watch over the nearby rebellious city of Soloi. The palace is connected with the main events in the adventurous history of Cyprus during the 5th century, when the Persians divided the kingdoms of the island between those who were pro-Greek and pro-Persian. The palace often changed hands, and its architecture echoes the political affiliation of its occupants. Apart from the royal apartments (once in the type of a Greek *megaron*, when the palace was controlled by a pro-Greek prince), there were also spacious store-rooms, reminiscent of Aegean palaces and several sanctuaries, the most famous being that of Athena (no.132). There were also advanced hygienic amenities, including bathrooms and one of the earliest systems of heating water for the bathroom. The palace, the only one of the classical period known in Cyprus, was excavated early in the 1930s by the Swedish Cyprus Expedition.

Bronze statuette of a cow from Vouni, cast
solid. It was found in one of the 'treasure
rooms' near the temple of Athena in the
palace of Vouni. The animal's attitude and the
rendering of the details are very realistic. This
statuette has been compared with the
well-known bronze statue of the Greek
sculptor Myron, which was famous for its
realism. It is dated to the middle of the 5th
century B.C.

Cyprus Museum, Nicosia. Excavations of
Vouni Palace (Swedish Cyprus Expedition),
no.152. Length: 19 cm.

129

Limestone funerary stele from Marion. The main part of the stele is decorated in low relief with a woman seated on a stool, wearing a chiton and a himation and holding in her left hand a bird which attracts her attention. The garments still retain some of their original blue paint. The upper part of the stele is decorated with voluted palmettes. The rendering of the facial characteristics of the seated woman, the rich folds of her garments, the hair-dressing, even the stool on which she is seated, copy features of Attic funerary stelae of the end of the 5th century B.C. (c.420 B.C.). Behind her head there is an engraved inscription in the Cypriot syllabary, in the Greek language, which reads: 'I am Aristila from Salamis, daughter of Onasis'.

Cyprus Museum, Nicosia, no.1957/III-18/1. Height: 92 cm.

130

Marble funerary stele from Marion. It
represents a nude young man in low relief. He
stands in front of a stele which bears an
engraved inscription in the Cypriot Greek
language, which reads: 'I am (the stele) of
Stases, the son of Stasioikos'. The face of the
young man, with its grave expression, recalls
the style of Attic funerary stelae. His mantle is
loose, covering only part of his left shoulder.
The rest serves as a background for the body;
originally it must have been painted. The
attitude of the arms and the fingers suggests
that he must have been playing a game, with
objects which may have been painted in the
background. As the rendering of the body is
somewhat provincial, it has been suggested
that this may be the work of a Cypriot artist
who was working under a strong influence
from Attic funerary monuments.

Cyprus Museum, Nicosia, no.1946/VII-28/1.
Height: 93.5 cm.

131

Terracotta moulded head of Heracles, from Kakopetria. He has a youthful, beardless face and wears a lion's skin on his head. This Greek hero was worshipped as a god in Cyprus and was often assimilated with the Phoenician god Melqart. At Kakopetria there was a sanctuary of Athena. The votive statuettes from the sanctuary, mostly in terracotta (though some were in limestone), were placed in a deposit (*bothros*); among them were some heads of Heracles, which suggest that the two deities shared the same sanctuary. This was often the case in Attica, as we know from the Greek traveller Pausanias.

Cyprus Museum, Nicosia. Excavations by the Cyprus Department of Antiquities at Kakopetria (1938), no.53. Height: 13 cm.

132

Small limestone head of Athena wearing a Greek helmet, from the sanctuary of Athena, Palace of Vouni (see no.127).
The worship of the goddess Athena was introduced to Cyprus in the 5th century B.C., at a time when national feeling on the island was high, a result of the wars of independence against the Persians. The goddess had sanctuaries in Vouni Palace at Soloi, and at Idalion.

5th century B.C. Cyprus Museum, Nicosia. Excavations at Vouni by the Swedish Cyprus Expedition, no.210. Height: 10.5 cm.

133

Marble head of Aphrodite, from Cyprus. This is one of the rare works of Greek classical sculpture in pentelic marble found in Cyprus. It represents Aphrodite (or Hygeia), in a style which recalls Greek sculpture of the beginning of the 4th century B.C. At this time, Greek sculptors must have been working in Cyprus, particularly in the court of Evagoras, pro-Greek king of Salamis. The head was found in the Gymnasium of Salamis, where it was used as building material in an Early Christian wall.

Cyprus Museum, Nicosia. Salamis Sculptures (Excavations by the Cyprus Department of Antiquities 1952), no.2.245. Height: 31.2 cm.

XI. A UNITED CYPRUS UNDER THE PTOLEMIES

A political and cultural seismic wave of considerable impact swept through the ancient world when a young Macedonian named Alexander led armies into Asia. The sweeping victories of the man known as "Alexander the Great" and the subsequent defeat of Persian armies brought hope to the pro-Greek kings of Cyprus. Even the Phoenician king of Kition sent Alexander a sword as a gift while Alexander was besieging Tyre.

The other Cypriot kings took an active part in the siege, donating 100 ships to the Greek cause. In appreciation, Alexander freed the Cypriot kingdoms from Persian rule and began unifying the island under a central government. Such unity, however, proved to be brief, for soon after Alexander's untimely death, Cyprus became the bone of contention between the two main successors of Alexander, his generals Ptolemy and Antigonus.

A victim of this antagonism was the last king of Salamis, Nicocreon, whose tragic story was narrated by the Greek author Diodorus. Ptolemy, having trusted the false accusations that Nicocreon was plotting against him, sent an army to take Salamis. Rather than fall into the hands of his enemy, Nicocreon and queen Axiothea, as well as all the members of the royal family, committed suicide.

Several years after this event, which took place in c. 311 B.C., Antigonus' son Demetrios Poliorketes, who ruled Cyprus after defeating Ptolemy, ordered that all those killed in the wars between his supporters and those of Ptolemy be buried. It must have been at this time (c. 306 B.C.) that Nicocreon and the other members of the royal family were given a magnificent funeral. A cenotaph, a rectangular stepped platform made of mud bricks on an elevated rocky base, was erected on a plain west of Salamis. A funeral pyre was set on the cenotaph. Then the monument, together with the remains of the pyre, and all the gifts (spears, shields, perfume bottles, etc.) were buried under a *tumulus* of earth.

Among the gifts were several clay human heads moulded on wooden poles. The "bodies" were carelessly rendered, doubtless because they were draped. It is probable that the heads wore crowns of gold or gilded bronze, and scholars suggest that some of the heads were actually portraits of the royal family, whose bodies, buried under the débris of their palace, could not be retrieved. Lending credence to this theory is the fact that two of the heads bear the realistic features of elderly persons, while the heads of a young woman and two male youths are idealised.

All the heads are rendered in the style of the great Greek sculptor Lysippos, who lived during the second half of the 4th century B.C. and who is known to have executed a portrait of Alexander the Great. The offerings and the statues (which must have been of unbaked clay which was hardened near the fire at the time of the ceremony) were piled up in a small conical mound at the end of the funerary ceremony and a large *tumulus* of earth was erected above them, which also covered the mud brick platform. The latter was placed off-centre so as to deceive prospective looters, as in fact it did.

The Nicocreon cenotaph, topped by a number of stone catapults, perhaps placed purposely by Demetrios Poliorketes, remained a landmark on the Salamis plain for many years. Looters and archaeologists alike tried unsuccessfully to excavate it. Not until 1964 was the ceremonial platform uncovered, fittingly enough, by the Cyprus Department of Antiquities.

The intrigues and conflicts of the two rival successors of Alexander the Great that had caused the death of king Nicocreon continued. Finally, Cyprus was absorbed by Ptolemy, who became king of Egypt and Cyprus. The island's 10 kingdoms were abolished, a single state was formed under unified civil and military commands, and Ptolemaic coinage became legal tender throughout the island.

This was the beginning of a new era of peace but not of prosperity, as the Ptolemies exploited Cyprus' wealth of copper and timber (used for ship-building) as well as other natural resources like corn. Their rule was very rigid. They appointed a military governor and a number of specialised officers, including one for the administration of the copper mines.

During this period, cultural life in the various cities centred around gymnasia, educational institutions which trained the mind and the body. Gymnasia were established by Alexander's officers, who found themselves in the East without Greek tutors for their children. Most of the major cities of Cyprus had such gymnasia as is known from inscriptions. Wealthy citizens contributed to the expenses related to the maintenance of the gymnasia.

With the decline of free political life in the cities, energy was channelled into gymnasia and other non-political interests like theatrical, musical and athletic contests, which served to raise the cultural standard of various cities. Art was not neglected. Though Cypriot art lost its originality and depended entirely on the common styles of Hellenistic art, Cypriot artists created some interesting pieces of sculpture and proved skilful in crafts like jewellery-making. But the individuality of Cypriot culture was over. Cyprus became a Ptolemaic province and followed artistic styles developed mainly in Alexandria, the capital of the new Ptolemaic kingdom.

However, Salamis, the island's capital for almost 1,000 years, retained its importance as a city of wealth and culture, despite the fact that in the 1st century B.C., the capital was transferred to *Nea* (New) Paphos, a town which was built round a natural harbour in the 4th century B.C.

Greek gods continued to be worshipped on the entire island, but a new element was introduced — the cult of the Ptolemaic ruler, which was organised by a specially-established association known as the "Confederation of the Cypriots". There were three main religious centres in Cyprus, which retained their importance down to the end of the Roman period: the temple of Aphrodite at Paphos (that of Kition was burnt by Ptolemy I in 312 B.C. after he had abolished the Phoenician dynasty of that city); the temple of Apollo of the Woods at Kourion; and the temple of Zeus at Salamis. Egyptian gods like Osiris, Sarapis and Isis were introduced by the Ptolemies and supplemented the Cypriot pantheon.

Funerary architecture became ostentatiously monumental. Ordinary rock-cut tombs consisted of a stepped *dromos* and multiple chambers with numerous niches for family burials. At Nea Paphos rock-cut tombs of a new type, imitating Alexandrine funerary architecture, appeared. They consisted of a large rectangular peristyle court with chambers and niches behind colonnaded porticos. These elaborate tombs were misnamed the "Tombs of the Kings". But they most probably belonged to rich Paphians or high officials of the state.

There must have been Greek-style temples, as is suggested by a marble frieze representing an Amazonomachy (a battle between the Greeks and Amazons) from Soloi, but none have survived. The great temple of Zeus at Salamis, whose podium was uncovered during recent excavations, is very impressive for its size and the dimensions of its stone columns and Corinthian capitals.

134

Silver coin of Paphos. King Stasandros. Middle of the 5th century B.C. On the obverse is a bull; on the reverse a flying eagle.

Cyprus Museum, Nicosia. Diameter: 2 cm.

135

Silver coin of Marion. King Timocharis. Second half of the 5th century. On the obverse a wreathed head of Apollo; on the reverse, Europa on a bull.

Cyprus Museum, Nicosia. Diameter: 2.3 cm.

The 10 kingdoms of Cyprus issued their own coinage, on the model of the Greek city-states. The first to issue such coinage was King Evelthon of Salamis (c.560-525 B.C.). The dies used for the coinage of the Cypriot kingdoms must have been made by Greek artists. They usually represent, on their obverse, gods and heroes of Greek mythology. The legends are in the Cypriot syllabary; the Greek alphabet was not introduced until the 4th century B.C. The earliest coinage is in silver and copper; gold coins were issued for the first time by Evagoras I, king of Salamis (411-374/3 B.C.). It was the prerogative of the Persian king to issue gold coins, and this action of Evagoras had a political meaning, since he considered himself equal to the king of Persia. During the reign of the Ptolemies, when Cyprus was unified under one ruler, coinage was issued for the whole of Cyprus.

136
Gold coin of Kition. King Baalmelek (425-400
B.C.). On the obverse Herakles (Melqart)
holding a bow and brandishing a club.

Cyprus Museum, Nicosia. Diameter: 1.2 cm.

137
Gold coin of Salamis. King Nicocles (373-c.361
B.C.). On the obverse a crowned head of
Aphrodite; on the reverse the head of Athena
wearing a Corinthian helmet.

Cyprus Museum, Nicosia. Diameter: 0.9 cm.

138

Clay portrait head, from the cenotaph of Nicocreon (Tomb 77) at Salamis. This head, together with others, male and female, was found on the platform of the cenotaph of Nicocreon, the last king of Salamis, who, according to historical information, committed suicide in 311 B.C. and, together with other members of the royal family, was buried under the burnt ruins of his palace. Probably several years afterwards the Salaminians built a cenotaph in their honour and offered them a pyre. They erected the portrait heads of the royal family round the pyre., These were made of unbaked clay which was moulded round wooden poles. The clay was hardened as a result of the pyre. The head illustrated here has accentuated facial characteristics. The mouth is half-open and the eyebrows are double-curved. There are traces of red paint on the face.

Cyprus Museum, Nicosia. Salamis Tomb 77, no.l347. Height: 16 cm.

139
Clay head of a woman, with idealised facial
characteristics, from the cenotaph of King
Nicocreon of Salamis (no.138). This is the only
female head found in the debris of the pyre.
Of the other heads found, two were portraits
of elderly men and two of young men, also
idealised. They indicate influences from the
Greek sculptor Lysippos, the artist who made
the portraits of Alexander the Great.

Cyprus Museum, Nicosia. Salamis Tomb 77,
no.870. Height: 26 cm.

140

Limestone head of a female figure, from Arsos. She wears a veil, which allows the filetted hair above the forehead to show, and ear-rings. The facial expression betrays strong influences from Hellenistic sculpture of the 3rd century B.C. There was a temple of Aphrodite at Arsos and the head may have belonged to a statue of this goddess.

Cyprus Museum, Nicosia. Cyprus Museum excavations at Arsos, no. 282. Height: 27 cm.

XII. CYPRUS UNDER THE ROMANS: THE END OF ANTIQUITY

The Ptolemies ruled Egypt and Cyprus for more than 200 years. The last decades of their rule, however, were not happy ones. Their authority was diminished as a result of intrigues and jealousies within the royal family. In their weakened state, the Ptolemies could not face a newly-emergent world power: the Romans, who struck the final blow against Ptolemaic presence in Cyprus in 67 B.C. Ironically, a trivial incident served as a pretext for their intervention, which subsequently led to their declaring the island part of the Roman empire.

The Romans claimed that the patrician Clodius Pulcher, who had been captured by pirates in Cypriot waters, was not ransomed properly (actually, the pirates let Clodius go free). Rome also claimed to possess a "will" left by the Ptolemy of Cyprus which ceded the island to Rome. Acting on these two "affronts", Rome annexed Cyprus. Administered by Cato as a province of Cilicia, Cyprus was bled by onerous taxes and by levies which stripped the island of much of its wealth.

Roman rule depended entirely on the disposition of the emperor towards the Cypriots. While the Romans proved to be mostly cruel rulers, there were emperors who favoured Cypriot cities, especially after natural disasters like the earthquakes of 15 B.C. and 77 A.D. Augustus, Trajan and Hadrian showed much interest in Cyprus and contributed towards the reconstruction of public buildings, particularly at Paphos and Salamis.

A seminal event occurred on Cyprus — in the face of Imperial Roman might — in 45 A.D. In this year, Christian missionaries including St. Barnabas, who was born on Cyprus, visited the island with the intent of converting the population there to the new religion of Christianity. Not only were the Cypriots converted, but the missionaries journeyed to the capital at New Paphos, where they converted the Roman proconsul,thus making Cyprus the first country in the world to be governed by a Christian ruler.

New Paphos continued to be the island's capital and its importance grew as a result of the prestige of the temple of Aphrodite at nearby Old Paphos. The presence of a powerful pagan temple at this time was reflective of the fact that the island as a whole did not succumb to Christianity quickly; indeed, Paul himself was eventually martyred for his efforts. Nonetheless, the city prospered. Its mint was responsible for all the coins used on the island. These coins, issued by the "Confederation of the Cypriots", show on the obverse the temple of Aphrodite. Some also show the statue of Salaminian Zeus, another indication of the city's importance. The legends on the coins, as well as all official decrees and dedicatory inscriptions, are in Greek, which was the official language of state in the Eastern provinces of the Roman empire.

The Greek geographer Strabo praised the city's imposing, well-built sanctuaries. A few of these buildings have been uncovered during recent excavations, but their state of preservation is very poor, as a result of continuous stone-robbing in the area for the construction of structures in medieval Paphos that included Byzantine churches. Something of the old splendour, however, may be seen in monuments like the Agora, the "Asklepeion" (or temple of Asklepios), the Odeon, and particularly two spacious and exceptional Roman villas. The largest of these villas, known as the "House of Theseus", is thought to be the palace of the Roman governor, because of its size and opulence. It was decorated with polychrome mosaic floors and painted walls. Its rooms and corridors contained marble statues of Greek gods, goddesses and heroes. These statues were found during recent excavations.

The best-known mosaic floors are within a circular "labirynth". Theseus, a hero of Greek mythology, occupies the central part of the circle, and is surrounded by other figures associated with the myth. These figures include the personification of Crete and the Minotaur; their names are shown in Greek capital letters. While this is a fine 3rd century A.D. mosaic with later repairs, the villa itself was in use as late as the 5th century A.D., and from this later period another mosaic floor has been preserved. It shows the preparations for the bath of the baby Achilles in the presence of his parents Peleus and Thetis, as well as the three Fates.

The second villa is known as the "House of Dionysus", because of the dionysiac themes depicted on some of its mosaic floors. Apart from the procession of Dionysus, which occupies a long panel, other panels depict themes from Greek mythology, such as the love story of Pyramus and Thisbe; the chasing of Daphne by the god Apollo; and of the nymph Amymone by Poseidon. Also of interest is an unusual mythological scene depicting the king of Attica, Ikarios, Dionysus and Acme. Dionysus, according to the myth, was entertained once by Ikarios and the former, in order to please his host, taught him the art of making wine. Ikarios is shown in the mosaic composition carrying wine-filled skins in his cart.

If New Paphos was the splendour of Cyprus during Roman rule, Salamis was her largest and most cosmopolitan centre. Salamis was inhabited by Greeks, Romans and Jews, but the common language of all of them was Greek, as it can be seen from numerous inscriptions found in ruined public buildings. Though it is difficult to calculate Salamis' population, an indication has been given by ancient authors. As a result of a Jewish revolt in 116 A.D., it was reported that 240,000 people were killed. Even if this figure is grossly exaggerated, one may safely say that the population of ancient Salamis, at least during the Roman period, was larger than any of the modern towns on Cyprus to-day. The town's theatre alone, which was rebuilt after the earthquakes of 15 B.C., had a capacity of 15,000 spectators and was at the time one of the largest in the ancient world. Its stage building was adorned with marble statues of the Muses and of their leader Apollo the lyre-player. Some of these statues have been discovered under the débris of the stage building, together with inscribed slabs naming the benefactors of the city, among whom was the emperor Hadrian.

The northernmost section of Salamis was the "cultural centre" of the Roman city. Apart from the theatre, there was a gymnasium, an amphitheatre, a stadium and spacious baths. The gymnasium, as already mentioned, had been built in the Hellenistic period and was enlarged after the earthquakes of 77 A.D., with the help of the emperors Hadrian and Trajan. The porticos round the palaestra of the gymnasium were adorned with large-size marble statues of Greek gods and heroes, while the various rooms of the baths contained large niches with wall mosaics, some of which are still well preserved.

Other public buildings which have been partly uncovered in the central part of Salamis are a large forum with granite columns and a vaulted water reservoir where water was stored after flowing through a monumental aqueduct from Kythrea, 30 miles west of Salamis.

Kourion, built on a rocky plateau, was also embellished with public buildings, including a theatre, which has been uncovered and restored. It was originally built in the 2nd century B.C., but was remodelled and enlarged in the 2nd century A.D. At a later time it was used for gladiatorial games, which were popular in Kourion. The floors of a nearby 3rd century A.D. villa are decorated with mosaics depicting scenes from the arena.

The remains of a stadium 233 m. long have been uncovered to the west of Kourion. The most important remains outside the town proper are those of the sanctuary of Apollo of the Woods. The sanctuary site was surrounded by a wall with gates, one gate facing Kourion, the other facing Paphos. Both gates no doubt connected with corresponding roads. Aside from the small podium temple with a paved "sacred street" leading to it, there were other buildings within the walled area, which comprised a palaestra, baths, a "hostel" for visitors, and store-rooms for gifts offered by worshippers. The latter could spend the night at the sanctuary site, which was one of the most famous on the island. A recently-discovered feature in the sanctuary area is a ring-shaped paved floor which was probably used for dancing. Within the ring are pits, perhaps meant for sacred trees, as ritual dances round such trees were known to have occurred on Cyprus from very early times.

Soloi, on the northern coast of the island, also was a flourishing city during the Roman period. Public buldings unearthed here include a theatre and a colonnaded paved street leading to an agora and a nympheum. Recent excavations have begun at Amathus, a southern town on the coast. On the acropolis, the remains of a large public building have begun to emerge. This is probably the temple of Aphrodite, since it fits the description and location of a temple given by ancient authors. In the lower city, a large paved area with a rectangular platform in the middle has been uncovered. Perhaps this was an altar or a podium for statues.

We know that a large number of other towns and townships in Cyprus flourished during the Roman period, but as yet, no excavations have been carried out. These were either descendants of towns which existed well before the Romans came, such as Kyrenia, Lapithos and Chytroi, or were new towns like Urania, Lafkolla, Tremithous and Drepanon. They belong to regional schools of sculpture, such as those of Asia Minor, a region which also influenced the architecture of public buildings on the island.

Art flourished on Roman-dominated Cyprus, as attested to by the fact that numerous statues were found in public buildings. They represent gods and heroes of Greek mythology. Official art is also represented, with larger than life-size statues of cuirassed emperors like those found at Salamis. Bronze statues are rare, but Cyprus produced one of the most striking and best known: an over life-size depiction of the emperor Septimius Severus. The artist decided to show him nude and athletic. He also included a fine portrait head. The bronze head of a youth of the Antonine period was found at Soloi, and one of Claudius, at Salamis.

141

Aerial view of the northernmost part of Salamis, on the east coast of Cyprus, where the Cyprus Department of Antiquities carried out extensive excavations from 1952 to 1974 and uncovered a number of public buildings of the Roman period. On the left is a spacious gymnasium (a school for the training of the mind and of the body) with a colonnaded palaestra (uncovered courtyard for athletic games) and an elaborate bathing establishment with bathrooms and swimming pools. On the extreme right is a theatre, one of the largest in the Eastern Mediterranean. Its stage building was decorated with marble statues of the Muses and their leader Apollo, playing the lyre. Between the gymnasium and the theatre there was a stadium and an amphitheatre (for gladiatorial games). There is also a complex of public baths in the vicinity. Salamis was very much favoured by the Roman emperors Trajan and Hadrian, who helped to reconstruct such public buildings after their destruction by earthquakes.

Aerial view of the sanctuary of Apollo at Kourion, west of the city site. The sanctuary, in honour of Apollo Hylates (of the woods), was first built in the 8th century B.C. and continued functioning down to the end of the Roman period (see no.110). Its present state dates to the Roman period. Apart from the actual temple, access to which was through a paved sacred street, there were also dormitories, store-rooms for the storing of offerings, bathrooms, a palaestra, etc. The whole sacred area was walled and had two gates, one on the west (Paphos gate) and the other on the east (Kourion gate), which no doubt corresponds with roads leading to Paphos and Kourion respectively. Pilgrims could stay overnight at the sanctuary. This was one of the three most important sanctuaries in Cyprus, together with the temple of Aphrodite at Paphos and that of Zeus at Salamis. All three had the privilege of the *asylum* (where persecuted persons could take refuge). The site is being excavated by an American mission, which continues earlier American excavations.

Aerial view of the site of Kourion, on the south coast of Cyprus. At the central part of the photograph one may see the theatre, and to the north-east the 'House of Eustolios'. The theatre was originally built in the 2nd century B.C.; when it was enlarged in the 2nd century A.D, it was transformed into an amphitheatre for gladiatorial games, and was turned into a theatre again at the end of the 3rd century A.D. It has now been partly restored for cultural performances. The 'House of Eustolios' was a private villa of a rich citizen of Kourion, built at the time of the transition from paganism to Christianity. The ascendancy of the Christian religion is manifested by the inscriptions on the mosaic floors of the various halls of the house, which refer to the triumph of Christ. The floors of the house are supplied with baths and are decorated with polychrome mosaics. The Department of Antiquities has excavated in recent years a villa of the late Roman period, one room of which is decorated with a mosaic floor representing gladiators, and is now in the course of excavating a large public building, perhaps a gymnasium, of the Roman period. There is also a spacious Early Christian Basilica on the site. The Acropolis of Kourion, as the above site is known, is built on top of a rocky plateau, the northern sides of which are cut vertically to replace a defensive wall.

144
A limestone portrait of the first century A.D.
The head is life-size and has accentuated facial
characteristics. It may be the portrait of the
Roman emperor Caligula (37-41 A.D.).

Cyprus Museum, Nicosia, no.1948/V-14/5.
Height: 25.5 cm.

145
Bronze head of a young man, from Soloi. The
head is over life-size and is characteristic of
the style of the Antonine period.

Cyprus Museum, Nicosia. Excavations by the
Université Laval, Québec, no.A13.
Height: 40 cm.

187

146
Marble statue of a nude Aphrodite from Soloi.
Her arms and the lower part of her legs are
missing. Her attitude recalls that of the type of
the Aphrodite of Cyrene.

First century B.C. Cyprus Museum, Nicosia,
no.E.510. Height: 81 cm.

147
Mosaic floor of a circular room of the House
of Theseus at Nea Paphos. In the centre of the
composition stands Theseus, the Athenian
hero who, according to legend, freed the
Athenian maidens from the Cretan Labyrinth,
having conquered the Minotaur. He managed
to get out of the Labyrinth with the help of
Ariadne. All the *dramatis personae* of the myth
are depicted round him. Crete and Ariadne
appear behind hillocks at the upper level, on
either side of Theseus. The Labyrinth
(personified) and the Minotaur lie near
Theseus' feet. There is a 'labyrinth' of
guilloches and other abstract patterns all
round the composition.

Villa of Theseus, Nea Paphos. Excavations by a
Polish mission. 3rd century A.D.

148

Two mosaic panels from a Roman villa at Nea Paphos, known as the 'House of Dionysus' because of the dionysiac scenes depicted on the mosaic floors of the various rooms of the villa. The mosaic panel on the left, which forms part of the floor of the western portico of the atrium, represents the love story of Pyramus and Thisbe which is narrated by Ovid. The lovers arranged to meet secretly, since their parents would not let them see each other. Thisbe was frightened by a lion (here a panther), dropped her cloak and ran away; the lion picked up the cloak in its mouth. When Pyramus saw the blood-stained cloak, thinking that Thisbe was dead, he killed himself in despair. When Thisbe found his dead body she did the same. In this panel, Thisbe, on the left, is seen running away, frightened; Pyramus is reclining, holding a cornucopia, as a young river-god. Between the two, and above, is a panther with Thisbe's cloak in its mouth.

149

The mosaic panel on the right forms part of the western portico of the atrium of the 'House of Dionysus'. It depicts the story of Daphne, the daughter of the river god Peneios (here on the extreme left). The god Apollo fell in love with her, but she wouldn't respond, and he pursued her. She is shown here fleeing from him. She prayed for help and was turned into a tree that bears her name (Daphne laurel). The young girl is shown here in the middle; her legs have already become part of a tree. The god, with his bow in his left hand, is shown on the right.

Nea Paphos. Excavations by the Cyprus Department of Antiquities. 3rd century A.D.

150

Mosaic floor from a late Roman building at Kourion. It represents two fully armed gladiators. Their Greek names (Margareites and Ellenikos) are written in Greek capital letters above their heads. The same villa produced other mosaic panels with a similar theme. It seems that gladiatorial games were favoured at Kourion during the Roman period. We know that the city's theatre was turned into an arena c.200 A.D.

Kourion, the Acropolis. Excavations by the Cyprus Department of Antiquities.

151

Wall painting in a semi-dome above the entrance to the central hall of the baths at the Salamis gymnasium. It represents an episode from the story of Hylas, the young friend of Heracles, who was sent to fetch water from a spring. The Nymph of the spring tried to lure him into her grotto, but he refused. Here Hylas (on the left) is shown standing behind a hillock, saying 'no' with a gesture of his right hand. The Nymph is seen on the right, with water pouring from her right hand. This is one of the earliest pictorial wall paintings found in Cyprus.

Salamis Gymnasium. Excavations by the Cyprus Department of Antiquities.
3rd century A.D.

A rectangular mosaic panel representing Leda and the Swan, from Palaepaphos. It formed the central pictorial panel of the mosaic floor of a room in a large Roman house or villa. The rest of the mosaic floor was decorated with abstract motifs. The panel is one metre square and is rendered in rich polychromes. Leda is seen from the back, stepping out of a lake or river, and walks towards a fountain, round which there are trees. The back of her body is seen in three-quarter view. She turns her head back to look at the Swan who moves in the opposite direction; its head is turned to play with Leda's garment which is very loose, and covers only her legs, leaving the largest part of her back exposed. There is grace and delicacy in the treatment of the figures and in the use of the colours. This composition is a well-known scene from Hellenistic and Roman art, illustrating the encounter of Leda with Zeus in the guise of a Swan. It may date to the first half of the 3rd century A.D.

Formerly in the Palaepaphos Museum, now in the Cyprus Museum, Nicosia. Excavations by the Swiss-German mission, 1972.

XIII. EPILOGUE

XIII. EPILOGUE: THE COMING OF CHRISTIANITY

Two successive earthquakes, in 332 and 342 A.D., destroyed the ancient cities of Cyprus, their public buildings and pagan temples. The impoverished population was not in a position to restore these cities to their ancient glory. Furthermore, the new religion of Christianity, which had by now planted secure roots among the Cypriots and even among the Romans, altered the cultural climate on Cyprus. At Kourion, the artist who decorated the mosaic floors of a 4th-5th century A.D. villa, known as the "House of Eustolios", described in Greek verse on the edge of the floor of a room the new cultural atmosphere that prevailed. Apollo no longer had a place there, nor did pagan statues; it was a time for Christ and Christian virtues.

It should be mentioned that the "House of Eustolios" was a luxurious one even so, as it was supplied with bath-rooms, and other rooms decorated with polychrome mosaics, one of which depicts "Construction" as a woman holding a measuring instrument.

Salamis was reconstructed during this period, but the new Christian city was much smaller than the old pagan one. It was renamed Constantia, after the Christian emperor Constantius, who aided the inhabitants by lifting taxes. Some of the public buildings outside the perimeter of the walls of the city were also restored, but in order to serve different purposes than those for which they were originally constructed. The palaestra of the gymnasium was paved to serve as a meeting place, and some of the statues of pagan gods were tolerated and re-erected to embellish the porticos, as long as they had been carefully mutilated according to the new Christian code of morality by removing their genitals. Even the baths in the gymnasium were restored — further proof that the transition from the comfortable life of the Roman period to the Christian way of life did not always involve asceticism. But while the stage of the theatre was partly restored for mimic productions, and other buildings were re-opened, pagan life with its glorious monuments belonged to the past.

The monuments of the new era were splendid basilicas, constructed with materials taken from nearby pagan buildings. Dedicated to the glory of God, the buildings were highly decorated with vivid mural paintings and mosaics. Many of these structures and their art works survive today as hallmarks of the Byzantine period of Cypriot history, which spanned in time the waning days of the Roman empire and the Third Crusade of Richard Coeur de Lion (1191), who like so many others before him, bent Cyprus to his will.

Thus, with a flourish, the curtain was lowered on the world of ancient Cyprus. It had lasted more than 7,000 years — a sweeping period of history that had seen numerous actors command and then leave the stage. But their dramas were filled with high adventure and political intrigue; and they left behind them vast storehouses of art, artefacts and architecture which enrich our lives today.

BIBLIOGRAPHY

Acts of the 1st International Congress of Cypriot Studies,
Nicosia 1969. Vol. I. Nicosia 1972.

Acts of the International Archaeological Symposium 'The Mycenaeans in the Eastern Mediterranean'. Nicosia 1973.

Acts of the International Archaeological Symposium 'The relations between Cyprus and Crete, ca.2000-500 B.C.'. Nicosia 1979.

ÅSTRÖM, P.: *The Middle Cypriote Bronze Age, The Late Cypriote Bronze Age, The Swedish Cyprus Exepedition,* vol. IV (IB-ID). Lund 1972.

ÅSTRÖM, P. AND OTHERS: *Hala Sultan Tekke I. Excavations 1897-1971.* (SIMA XLV:1). Göteborg 1976.

BENSON, J. L.: *The Necropolis of Kaloriziki* (SIMA XXXVI). Göteborg 1973.

BENSON, J. L.: *Bamboula at Kourion.* Pennsylvania, Philadelphia 1972.

BIRMINGHAM, J. (Ed): 'The Cypriote Bronze Age' *Australian Studies in Archaeology,* no.1 (1973).

BOARDMAN, J.: *The Greeks overseas* (revised edit.). London 1980.

BROWN, A. C. - CATLING, H. W.: *Ancient Cyprus.* Oxford 1975.

BUCHHOLZ, H. - G. & KARAGEORGHIS, V.: *Altägäis und Altkypros.* Tübingen 1971.

CASSON, S.: *Ancient Cyprus.* London 1937.

CATLING, H. W.: *Cypriot Bronzework in the Mycenaean World.* Oxford 1964.

CATLING, H. W.: 'Cyprus in the Neolithic and Bronze Age Periods', *Cambridge Ancient History* (3rd. rev. edit. vols I-II, Pts 1-2). Cambridge 1970-71.

CHAVANE, M.-J. & YON, M.: *Testimonia Salaminia* 1 (Salamine de Chypre X). Paris 1978.

CHEAL, C. L.: *Early Hellenistic Architecture and Sculpture in Cyprus: Tumulus 77 at Salamis.* (Diss.) Ann Arbor, Michigan 1980.

COLDSTREAM, J. N.: *Geometric Greece.* London 1977.

COLEMAN, J. & BARLOW, J.: 'Cornell excavations at Alambra, 1978', *Report of the Department of Antiquities Cyprus,* 1979, 159ff.

COOK, B. F. (ed.): *Cypriote Art in the British Museum.* London 1979.

DESBOROUGH, V. R. d'A.: *The Last Mycenaeans and their Successors.* Oxford 1964.

DESBOROUGH, V. R. d'A.: *The Greek Dark Ages.* London 1972.

DES GAGNIERS, J. - KARAGEORGHIS, V.: *Vases et figurines de l'Age du Bronze à Chypre.* Québec 1976.

DESHAYES, J. L.: *La nécropole de Ktima.* Paris 1963.

DIKAIOS, P.: 'The excavations at Vounous-Bellapais in Cyprus, 1931-1932', *Archaeologia* 88 (1938), 1ff.

DIKAIOS, P.: *Khirokitia*. Oxford 1953.

DIKAIOS, P.: *Sotira*. Philadelphia 1961.

DIKAIOS, P.: *A guide to the Cyprus Museum*. (3rd edit.). Nicosia 1961.

DIKAIOS, P.: *Enkomi, Excavations 1948-1958*, vols I-III. Mainz 1969 and 1971.

DIKAIOS, P. & STEWART, J. R.: *The Stone Age and the Early Bronze Age in Cyprus* (The Swedish Cyprus Expedition, vol. IV (IA). Lund 1962.

FURUMARK, A.: *The Mycenaean pottery, Analysis and Classification*. Stockholm 1941.

GEORGHIOU, H.: 'Relations between Cyprus and the Near East in the Middle and Late Bronze Age', *Levant* XI (1979), 84ff.

GJERSTAD, E.: *Studies on Prehistoric Cyprus*. Uppsala 1926.

GJERSTAD, E.: *The Swedish Cyprus Expedition. Finds and Results of the Excavations in Cyprus 1927-1931*, vols I-III. Stockholm 1934-1937.

GJERSTAD, E.: *The Cypro-Geometric, Cypro-Archaic and Cypro-Classical Periods* (*The Swedish Cyprus Expedition* vol. IV(2). Stockholm 1948.

GJERSTAD, E.: 'The phoenician colonization and expansion in Cyprus', *Report of the Department of Antiquities Cyprus*, 1979, 230ff.

GJERSTAD, E.: 'The origin and chronology of the Early Bronze Age in Cyprus', *Report of the Department of Antiquities Cyprus*, 1980, 1ff.

HADJIOANNOU, K.: Ἡ Ἀρχαία Κύπρος εἰς τάς Ἑλληνικάς πηγάς. Τόμοι Α-Δ. Λευκωσία (1971-1980).

HILL, G. F.: *A Catalogue of the Greek Coins of Cyprus in the British Museum*. London 1904.

HILL, G. F.: *A History of Cyprus* I. Cambridge 1940.

KARAGEORGHIS, J.: *La grande déesse de Chypre et son culte*. Lyon 1977.

KARAGEORGHIS, V.: 'Chronique des fouilles et découvertes archéologiques à Chypre', *Bulletin de Correspondance Hellénique* since 1958 to the present day.

KARAGEORGHIS, V.: *Treasures in the Cyprus Museum*. Nicosia 1962.

KARAGEORGHIS, V.: *Mycenaean Art from Cyprus*. Nicosia 1963.

KARAGEORGHIS, V.: *Corpus Vasorum Antiquorum, Cyprus*. Fasc. I-II. Nicosia 1963 and 1965.

KARAGEORGHIS, V.: *Sculptures from Salamis*, I. Nicosia 1964.

KARAGEORGHIS, V.: *Nouveaux documents pour l'étude du Bronze Récent à Chypre* (Etudes Chypriotes III). Paris 1965.

KARAGEORGHIS, V.-VERMEULE, C. C.: *Sculptures from Salamis*, II. Nicosia 1966.

KARAGEORGHIS, V.: *Excavations in the Necropolis of Salamis*, I-IV. Nicosia 1967, 1970, 1973 and 1978.

KARAGEORGHIS, V.: *Cyprus* (Archaeologia Mundi). Geneva 1968.

KARAGEORGHIS, V.: *Salamis in Cyprus, Homeric, Hellenistic and Roman* (New Aspects of Antiquity). London 1969.

KARAGEORGHIS, V.: 'Notes on some Cypriote Priests', *Harvard Theological Review* 64 (1971), 261ff.

KARAGEORGHIS, V. AND OTHERS: 'Concerning two Mycenaean pictorial sherds from Kouklia (Palaepaphos) Cyprus', *Archäologischer Anzeiger* (1972), 188ff.

KARAGEORGHIS, V. AND OTHERS: *Excavations at Kition*, vols I-III. Nicosia 1974, 1976, 1977.

KARAGEORGHIS, V. - DES GAGNIERS, J.: *La céramique chypriote de style figuré* (Biblioteca di Antichità Cipriote 2). Roma 1974.

KARAGEORGHIS, V.: *Alaas. A protogeometric necropolis in Cyprus*. Nicosia 1975.

KARAGEORGHIS, V.: *The civilization of Prehistoric Cyprus*. Athens 1976.

KARAGEORGHIS, V.: *Kition, Mycenaean and Phoenician discoveries in Cyprus* (New Aspects of Antiquity). London 1976.

KARAGEORGHIS, V.: *Two Cypriote sanctuaries of the end of the Cypro-Archaic period*. Rome 1977.

KARAGEORGHIS, V. AND OTHERS: *Cypriote Antiquities in the Medelhavsmuseet Stockholm* (Memoir 2). Stockholm 1977.

KARAGEORGHIS, V.: *The goddess with uplifted arms in Cyprus*. (Scripta Minora 1977-78). Lund 1977.

KARAGEORGHIS, V.: 'Fouilles à l'Ancienne Paphos de Chypre. Les premiers colons Grecs', *Comptes Rendus de l'Académie des Inscriptions et Belles Lettres*, (1980), 121ff.

LE BRUN, A.: 'Cap Andréas Kastros, rapport préliminaire 1970-72', *Report of the Department of Antiquities Cyprus*, 1974, 1ff.

LE BRUN, A.: 'Khirokitia, rapport préliminaire sur la séconde campagne des fouilles 1977', *Report of the Department of Antiquities Cyprus*, 1978, 1ff.

MAIER, F.G.: 'Excavations at Kouklia Palaepaphos', *Report of the Department of Antiquities Cyprus*, (since 1967 to the present day).

MASSON, E.: *Cyprominoica. Répertoires, documents de Ras Shamra. Essais d'interprétation* (SIMA XXXI:2). Göteborg 1974.

MASSON, E.: 'A la recherche des vestiges Proche-Orientaux à Chypre', *Archäologischer Anzeiger* (1976), 139ff.

MASSON, O.: *Les Inscriptions Chypriotes Syllabiques* (Etudes Chypriotes I). Paris 1961.

MEIGGS, R.: 'Cyprus in the fifth century', *The Athenian Empire* (Appendix 7). Oxford 1972.

MELLAART, J.: *The Neolithic of the Near East*. London 1975.

MERRILLEES, R. S.: *Trade and Transcendence in the Bronze Age Levant* (SIMA XXXIX). Göteborg 1974.

MITFORD, T. B. & NICOLAOU, I.: *The Greek and Latin Inscriptions from Salamis* (Salamis vol. 6). Nicosia 1974.

NICOLAOU, I. & Mørkholm, O.: *Paphos I. A ptolemaic coin hoard*. Nicosia 1976.

NICOLAOU, K.: *Ancient Monuments of Cyprus*. Nicosia 1968.

NICOLAOU, K.: *The Historical Topography of Kition*. Göteborg 1976.

PECORELLA, P. E.: *Le tombe dell'età del Bronzo Tardo della necropoli a mare di Ayia Irini 'Paleokastro'* (Biblioteca di antichità cipriote 4:1). Rome 1977.

PELON, O.: *Tholoi, Tumuli et Cercles funéraires*. Paris 1976.

PELTENBURG, E. J.: 'Ayios Epiktitos Vrysi, Cyprus', *Proceedings of the Prehistoric Society* 41 (1975), 17ff.

PELTENBURG, E. J.: 'The Prehistory of West Cyprus. Ktima Lowlands. Investigations 1976-1978', *Report of the Department of Antiquities Cyprus*, 1979, 69ff.

PELTENBURG, E. J.: Lemba, Archaeological project, Cyprus, 1978', *Levant* XII (1980), 1ff.

PIERIDOU, A.: Ὁ Πρωτογεωμετρικός Ρυθμός ἐν Κύπρῳ. Ἀθῆναι 1973.

POPHAM, M. R. AND OTHERS (editors): *Lefkandi I*. London 1979-80.

POUILLOUX, J.: 'Salaminiens de Chypre à Délos', *Bulletin de Correspondance Hellénique* (Suppl. I: Etudes Déliennes). Paris 1973, 399ff.

POUILLOUX, J.: 'Chyptiotes à Delphes', *Report of the Department of Antiquities Cyprus* 1976, 158ff.

SALAMINE DE CHYPRE. Histoire et Archéologie. Colloque du CNRS no.578, Lyon 13-17 mars 1978. Paris 1980.

SANDARS, N. K.: *The Sea Peoples*. London 1978.

SCHACHERMEYR, F.: *Die ägäische Frühzeit*. Band 2: *Die Mykenische Zeit*. Wien 1976.

SCHAEFFER, C. F. A.: *Enkomi-Alasia* I. Paris 1952.

SCHAEFFER, C. F. A. & OTHERS: *Alasia* I. Paris 1971.

SJÖQVIST, E.: *Problems of the Late Cypriote Bronze Age*. Stockholm 1940.

SPYRIDAKIS, C.: Κύπριοι Βασιλεῖς τοῦ 4ου αἰ. π.Χ. (411-311/10 π.Χ.). Λευκωσία 1963.

STAGER, L. E. AND OTHERS: *American Expedition to Idalion, Cyprus. First preliminary report 1971-1972*. Cambridge-Massachusetts 1974.

STANLEY PRICE, N. P.: 'Khirokitia and the initial settlement of Cyprus', *Levant* IX (1977), 66f.

STANLEY PRICE, N.P.: 'The structure of settlement at Sotira in Cyprus', *Levant* XI (1979), 46ff.

STEWART, E. AND J. R.: *Vounous 1937-1938*. Lund 1950.

STILLWELL, R.: 'Kourion-The Theater', *Proceedings of the American Philosophical Society* 105 (1961), 37ff.

STUDIES presented in memory of Porphyrios Dikaios. Nicosia 1979.

TATTON-BROWN, V. (ed.): *Cyprus B.C. 7000 years of history*. London 1979.

TAYLOR, J. DU PLAT: *Myrtou-Pigadhes*. Oxford, 1957.

TODD, I. A.: 'Vasilikos valley project: First preliminary report, 1976', *Report of the Department of Antiquities Cyprus*, 1977, 5ff.

TODD, I. A.: 'Vasilikos valley project, 1977-1978: an interim report', *Report of the Department of Antiquities Cyprus*, 1979, 13ff.

VAGNETTI, L.: 'Figurines and minor objects from a Chalcolithic cemetery at Souskiou-Vathyrkakas (Cyprus)', *Studi Micenei ed Egeo-Anatolici* XXI (1980), 17ff.

VERMEULE, C. C.: *Greek and Roman Cyprus*. Boston 1976.

VERMEULE, E.: *Toumba tou Skourou. The mound of darkness*. Boston 1974.

VERMEULE, E. & KARAGEORGHIS, V.: *Mycenaean Pictorial vase-painting*. (1981).

VESSBERG, O. & WESTHOLM, A.: *The Hellenistic and Roman periods in Cyprus* (The Swedish Cyprus Expedition vol. IV(3). Stockholm 1956.

WATKINS, T.: 'Some problems of the Neolithic and Chalcolithic period in Cyprus', *Report of the Department of Antiquities Cyprus*, 1973, 34ff.

YON. M.: *La Tombe T. I du XIe s. av. J.-C.* (Salamine de Chypre II). Paris 1971.

YON, M.: *Un dépôt de sculptures archaïques* (Salamine de Chypre V). Paris 1974.

INDEX

Indexer: JOYCE ANDREWS

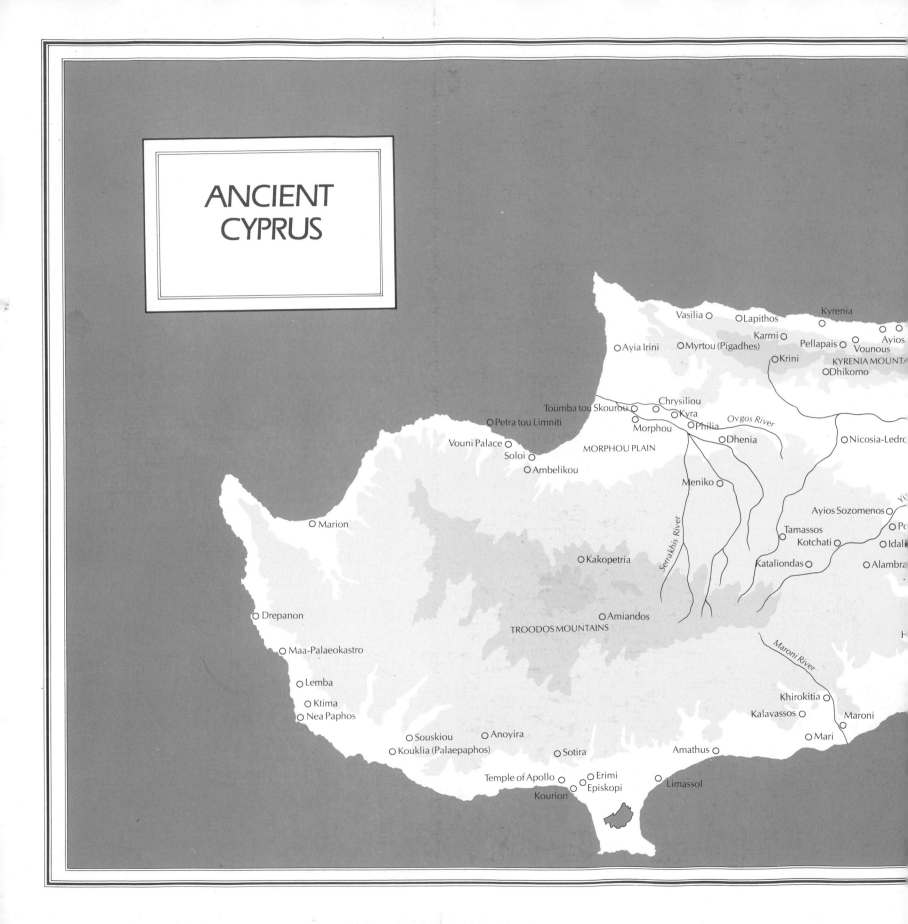

ANCIENT CYPRUS

Vasilia
Lapithos
Kyrenia
Karmi
Ayia Irini
Myrtou (Pigadhes)
Pellapais
Vounous
Ayios
Krini
KYRENIA MOUNTA
Dhikomo
Chrysiliou
Toumba tou Skourou
Kyra
Ovgos River
Petra tou Limniti
Philia
Morphou
Nicosia-Ledro
Vouni Palace
Dhenia
Soloi
MORPHOU PLAIN
Ambelikou
Meniko
Marion
Ayios Sozomenos
Tamassos
Po
Kotchati
Idal
Kakopetria
Kataliondas
Alambra
Serrakhis River
Drepanon
Amiandos
TROODOS MOUNTAINS
Maroni River
Maa-Palaeokastro
H
Lemba
Khirokitia
Ktima
Kalavassos
Maroni
Nea Paphos
Mari
Souskiou
Anoyira
Kouklia (Palaepaphos)
Sotira
Amathus
Temple of Apollo
Erimi
Limassol
Episkopi
Kourion